The Art of Learning Math

The Art of Learning Math

A Manual for Success

Susan Midlarsky

ROWMAN & LITTLEFIELD
Lanham • Boulder • New York • London

Published by Rowman & Littlefield
An imprint of The Rowman & Littlefield Publishing Group, Inc.
4501 Forbes Boulevard, Suite 200, Lanham, Maryland 20706
www.rowman.com

86-90 Paul Street, London EC2A 4NE, United Kingdom

British Library Cataloguing in Publication Information Available

Library of Congress Cataloging-in-Publication Data Available

ISBN 978-1-4758-7094-7 (cloth) | ISBN 978-1-4758-7095-4 (pbk) | ISBN 978-1-4758-7096-1 (epub)

Contents

Foreword

Dr. Yeap Ban Har

The Art of Learning Math: A Manual for Success looks at teaching math through the lenses of meaning, connection, and joy. It juxtaposes the author's personal and professional experiences in teaching and learning mathematics with research and learning theories to provide readers with suggestions and insights that can provide students with positive learning experiences in math.

Educators get to revisit math pedagogical content knowledge even as they make new connections and develop fresh insights. The book is also parent friendly, as technical jargon is used sparingly and thoroughly explained.

The progression from early childhood years to adulthood provides readers with an overview of how math ideas, concepts, and skills are meaningfully connected and how they relate to the learners' experiences. It encourages a growth mindset to escape any beliefs that the reader might have that they are unable to do math.

There are several facets to the art of learning math.

When students formally learn a topic, they are doing exactly that—formal learning. They probably already have some form of understanding of the idea under study. Young learners have experience with all their fingers numbering ten. This experience and the related everyday language allow students to understand the concept of renaming one *ten* as ten *ones*. Students make connections between their existing real-world experiences and mathematical concepts.

Concrete manipulatives, like toys for learning math, can be used for discovery of math concepts. Pattern blocks can be used to create pictures and develop understanding of part-whole relationships. Using square tiles to cover a surface, students connect their playful experience in fitting jigsaw puzzle pieces into a frame with the more structured classroom activity. This serves as a conduit for students to make sense of the formula used to calculate area of rectangles.

Another facet of the art of learning math is realizing the relationships between and among topics, including visually. Students who have learned the Pythagorean theorem can see that this can lead to a formula to calculate distance between two points on a Cartesian plane in coordinate geometry. Or the properties of angles at the center and angles at the circumference of a circle are easily proven using basic geometrical ideas learned in elementary school.

When younger students learn multiplication, they see $9 + 9 + 9$ and 3×9 as different expressions to describe the same situation. Making connections allow students to go deeper into the subject by building mental schemas rather than collections of isolated facts.

By making connections throughout, the book reveals the artistry of numbers, mathematics, and their meaning in life.

The chapters are filled with a treasury of examples and strategies that readers will find practical and ready for use. These specifics are organized around general math education principles that help readers understand the theoretical underpinnings behind the examples and strategies.

The Art of Learning Math: A Manual for Success can serve as a lens for readers to construct their personal knowledge about how students can learn math in a meaningful way. It brings to life what may have been paper and pencil concepts in the past, allowing readers to find new life and satisfaction in the understanding of what math is and how numbers work. It is a must-read in the library of anyone who wants to make math a more meaningful part of their life.

Introduction

There is no greater joy than that of a human connected to its nature and the patterns of the infinite universe.

When humans are born, they have an arduous journey ahead of them to make sense of the wonders of the natural world and the irrationality of the human-made world around them.

This book sets out to help the reader make sense of aspects of the natural world in connection with the human-made world, through the lens of mathematics.

To do so, we make a backward journey to a time before there were math books and professors, numerals and computers. All of those are layered upon the truth of what exists, but at such remote levels, and often so disconnected from the concepts, that many students of mathematics become lost in the morass of procedures and formulas.

Deeply knowledgeable and passionate math teachers will open cognitive and experiential doors to their students, so it all makes sense and is relevant. The art and beauty of it becomes clear as well. That's the effort of the many researchers and educators who have been trying to reform math education for decades. However, this meets centuries of habit ingrained by generation after generation of chalk-and-talk teaching, in which people become either "good or bad" at math.

This book demystifies some aspects of math and brings them to life. It aims to be a resource for teachers and homeschooling parents, for adults struggling to make sense of math, and for peoplewho want to ignite more of a passion for math than what they already have. For those with trauma relating to math education, it may provide paths to inspiration and self-healing about the subject as well.

As the reader reads through this book, there may be times when there are beliefs or personal history about math that create barriers against appreciating and enjoying math. For those times, try using the power of the word *yet*. For instance, instead of, "I don't like math," it could be, "I don't like math *yet*." Or instead of, "I can't understand this mathematical thinking," change it to, "I don't understand this mathematical thinking *yet*." This will leave the doors open for growth in your mind and provide more possibility for helping the child or children in your care.

At the end of each chapter, there is a bulleted set of ideas to put what you have learned into practice. These also summarize the main points in the chapter. Some people, especially busy teachers, may find it easier to start with the bulleted list and then read the extended content.

At times, especially in the later chapters, you may find that the math gets a bit technical or challenging to read through. Hang in there! Remember that it's challenging because you haven't understood it *yet*. You can either skate past those sections and return when you're ready, or you can slow down and patiently work through them with pencil and paper. Your perseverance will pay off.

What do you wish you would have had in your math education that would have provided a better foundation for your life today?

The author wishes that concepts would have been taught that made math meaningful from the start.

Chapter 1

Infancy

The Platform for Everything

An infant is an empty computer with endless possibilities.

Imagine being transported in a moment to a whole new planet, entering it painfully, and having little to no control of your new bodily functions, while you're completely at the mercy of caretakers. You know absolutely nothing about this place: you don't speak the language; you don't know the food and what you like or dislike; you don't know the colors or plants or animals or sounds, and what is dangerous or safe; and your communication abilities are extremely limited.

Not only that, but the body you are in is so sensitive and delicate that the smallest sensation feels huge to you. Light, sounds, tastes, smells, touch. Everything is brand new, and you have no control over almost anything except your voice. This is the experience of a human infant born into this world.

When a baby is born, it receives a deluge of intense, brand-new experiences. A mass of sensory input from inside and out, from sounds, smells, textures, sights, tastes, to sensations such as hunger, pain, pleasure, and more, impose themselves upon the fresh little life.

The baby's first few months are spent making neurological connections about anything and everything, but mostly about the family and the immediate experience of the infant. Of course, the baby's surroundings make a huge difference in its ability to make sense of the world. Those who have parents who patiently support the child's sense-making have an advantage over those who experience chaos or trauma, or who are bereft of caring experiences.

The main teacher for the infant at this stage is its own body. As they grow, babies explore the world through their senses. Any parent knows that anything and everything a baby touches is thoroughly explored, including in its mouth. That's why the mouth knows exactly what everything feels and tastes

1

like. Try it: look around the room you are in, and think about what it would be like to touch your tongue to each object. You know exactly how it will taste and feel!

The child also explores its own body while learning how to control it. A baby can spend hours looking at different parts of its body, interacting with fingers, touching feet, trying out movements, blowing bubbles, making sounds, and more.

Our hands are amazing things: starfish attached to the ends of movable, bendable rods (our arms) on our bodies. One teacher calls the fingers "magic counting sticks" with her students. Having these magic sticks, or fingers, on our bodies means that babies are able to recognize small quantities.

Consider the word *digit*. We use it all the time to mean a numeral in a place in a number. But it also means *finger*. The connection to the world of mathematics is right in front of us!

The development of counting varies but usually follows a specific progression. Infants can *subitize*, or recognize quantities up to one to three, without counting. The development of *cardinality*, or connecting a number of objects to a specific number, takes longer and follows the development of the counting sequence, or the ability to count, "One, two, three, four, five," and so forth.

This leads to what feel like "easy," or intuitive, numbers later in life. Most teachers know that the easiest counting sequences to understand are counting by ones, twos, fives, and tens. Counting by sevens can be quite tricky; try comparing that to counting by fives!

Look again at the hands. What is our experience? Humans (by vast majority) are born with two hands, five fingers on each hand, and ten fingers. This is why the base ten number system that we most commonly use is easiest for us to understand, and why the metric system is easier than the imperial system. It's also why the roman numeral system was so thoroughly overtaken by the Arabic numeral system.

As you interact with babies, talk to them about everything around them. Name objects, people, and actions. Take it slow and easy for good absorption; remember, they are like the aliens we described earlier, and everything is new and strange. As you do so, count objects, fingers, and so on, but only within five. This will give a jump start of familiarity with the counting sequence.

Songs with numbers and counting can be fun and helpful as well. Encourage babies to babble and later, sing along,[1] but don't expect them to understand number concepts based on that. That understanding will develop in time. Right now we're introducing how things work, making the unfamiliar less anxiety producing, and introducing numbers as a fun, achievable, enjoyable part of life.

Toys connected to math concepts can be helpful too, whether they are numbers of dots or shapes, or numerals themselves. With the focus on familiarity and comfort, this stage should be all about play. Learning the names of shapes can be part of a helpful foundation too, as many baby toys have shapes, and naming them can be part of play. Then the naming can extend to everyday objects, like calling a ball a sphere, round, and so on; pointing out rectangles on windows and books; noting the triangle of a bird's beak.

Part of the key here is for the adults to notice and enjoy these shapes as well, which will help the child to understand and learn about them comfortably. As the book proceeds, we'll see ways for this good relationship with math to grow in both children and adults.

IMPORTANT PRACTICES

- Talk to babies about everything around them.
- Count their fingers and toes out loud: one, two, three, four, five. (Keep the count within five; use each hand and each foot separately.)
- Introduce number and counting songs.
- Name shapes in their toys and in the world around them.
- Count things out loud when you are with them.
- Count the number of times they have dropped a specific thing—but without any impatience. Make it a game!
- Get age-appropriate numbered and math-related objects to play with, just for exposure to numerals and other concepts: blocks, 3D numbers, and so forth.

What do you wonder about an infant's experience that you still don't know?
The author wonders why our fingers aren't all the same lengths.

NOTE

1. Babies who are hard of hearing can learn the signs for the numbers.

Chapter 2

Early Childhood

Counting Development

Mathematics begins with what we can see, feel, and touch.

While a deep understanding of mathematics involves more than just the brain, understanding brain development can help guide mathematical understanding appropriately. Between ages one and four, a whole panorama of possibilities exists in brain development. This is a prime time to plant the seeds of possibility so that a child can have as many options available for their future as possible.

When babies are born, their brains are like a soup of possibility, rich with tens of millions of brain cells, or neurons, waiting to be connected together. Learning is the process of making connections between the neurons, called *synapses*, and later forming stable circuits of connection.[1]

Between ages two and three, children have their peak number of brain synapses, or connections, available for providing foundations for learning in the rest of their life. *Synaptic pruning* is a process in which extra neurons and unused synaptic connections are removed to increase efficiency in the brain. This process begins at around age two and continues at a high rate until about age ten, then continues to age twenty. As an aside, over- or underpruning may play a role in some abnormalities found in brains with schizophrenia, Alzheimer's, and other brain-related abnormalities.

Keeping the enormous possibilities of the young brain in mind, parents and caregivers can provide excellent foundations for number sense in early childhood. Many parents already do this by exposing their children to multiple languages, so why not numbers?

In number sense, the counting sequence comes first: being able to count one, two, three, four, five, up to ten. It's normal for young children to mix up the order of the numbers, because the numbers are just words at first. Playing games and singing songs with the number sequence up to ten can help with this sequencing. For example, Talking Hands Talking Feet has some songs such as "DRMD—Rhythm Door," "Five Come Alive," and "Count on Us" that promote gentle learning and early number sequencing.[2]

The earliest cardinality, or understanding the connection between number names and number of things, begins with an understanding of "one or more-than-one." In languages that have a different form for a plural of a noun than for the singular, such as an *s* in English for plurals, children tend to develop this cardinality more quickly than in languages that don't, like Japanese. This is one sign of the essential connection between language and number development in children. Therefore, the more parents and teachers count with children, the more the children's ability to count will develop.

As they get older, children develop the ability to count up to five objects. At first, if they start counting the objects, they have to start over if they are interrupted. As they develop a stronger sense of cardinality, they can carry on in spite of interruptions, and eventually they will not have to touch the objects in order to count them.[3]

Families and preschools can support cardinality by having fun counting things when out and about. In nature, count the number of petals and leaves on plants. Count the number of ducks on a lake. Count small numbers of everything! In cities, count how many train cars on the subway. Count how many cars of a certain color pass by. Count the eggs in a carton. Count how many traffic lights you drive through. Count the days in the week, the seasons, anything you can think of.

In these early years, it's important to keep the number of counted objects small, especially at first. Keeping it mostly within five for ages one to three and within ten for age four, with some exceptions, will help the child make the connection between the count and the objects. At age four, a calendar where every day is marked off as it comes, and/or a "One Hundred Days of School" chart, can also be helpful.

Model how to count things by touching or pointing and saying the number. If counting something abstract, like the seasons, track your numbers with both the number name and fingers: "Spring [index finger raised], summer [add the middle finger]," etc. This will help the child understand how to keep count using their "magic counting sticks."

Some researchers have found that a key part of grasping the number sequence is to develop a mental number line. Besides using the fingers to track numbers, even when just counting together one to ten, it can be helpful to play board games that involve moving a counter a certain number of spaces. This helps build an association between the mental number line and number of moves. It's also related to the fact that cardinality is associated with visual-spatial development.

The concept of "zero" is more advanced and doesn't need to be introduced yet; talking about "nothing" or "none left" can be useful, though. It's also important to let children experience the fun of counting and enumerating without pressure, meaning it's important to play with the numbers without the children being expected to perform or be quizzed on them. They can volunteer to count and show, though.

Traditionally, boys' games have had more visual-spatial elements to them, which may also help to explain why boys have found math more intuitive in the past. For example, boys traditionally play ball games, build with blocks and other toys, race cars, and so on. To even the playing field for all children, providing similar opportunities for all children can help. For example, playing games such as T-ball, where there are numbered bases, can help develop cardinality.

Other helpful mathematical foundations can be provided by playing with 3D shapes, recognizing positional attributes (above, below, higher, lower, near, far), and using comparison language (the same as, more than, less than). For example, talk about who is taller than whom in the family; take pictures of groceries purchased from week to week and compare how many groceries were purchased one week to the next ("Last week we bought *more* groceries than this week"); look at maps to discuss distance, plan trips (even across town), and compare the experience of those trips to how they looked on the map.

Similarly, pattern recognition is important to begin when children are young. Start conversations about patterns, like the black and white stripes on a crosswalk, the days in a week, the seasons, and so on. Invite questions and exploration of these patterns. "What do you notice about this? What do you think might come next? What might have come before?" These are some of the fundamentals of the science of mathematics.

It's important not to get too academic too soon, though. There are viral videos of parents teaching their children to make equations at age two or three using manipulatives with numbers and symbols on them. The problem with pushing academics too early is that it can cause learning to be too narrow and shallow, rather than allowing it to grow the deep roots and meaningful connections developed through play and movement that little concrete learners require.

IMPORTANT PRACTICES

- Count to ten in words and song.
- Count small numbers of lots of things: flower petals, leaves, cars, eggs, and so forth.

- Track the count of abstract things using fingers and the number sequence.
- Play games. Playing with dominoes, playing board games like Candyland and card games like War, and even counting coins can help children understand cardinality.
- Play with 3D shapes.
- Talk about positions of things or people.
- Use comparison language about different things.
- Don't quiz children or ask them to count or show numbers on their own at this stage.
- Don't push academic/abstract learning at this stage.

What do you wonder about this that you still don't know?

The author wonders how the concept of "zero," which changed so much of how we understand math, developed in human understanding.

NOTES

1. Visualization available at https://susanmidlarsky.com/neural-connections-a-visualization/.

2. Songs available at https://talkinghandstalkingfeet.com/songs/.

3. A good resource to learn more about this progression and help develop this counting is Char Forsten and Torri Richards, *Math Talk: Teaching Concepts & Skills through Illustrations & Stories* (Peterborough, NH: Crystal Springs Books, 2009).

Chapter 3

Middle Childhood

The Big Adventure

Almost all the math I use as an adult, I learned in elementary school.

Elementary school, or grades kindergarten through five (ages five to ten), is when most people either feel like they are comfortable with math or else begin to develop fears about math. This is highly dependent upon teachers, the messages received from parents, and society's views about math in general.

MINDSET AND IDENTITY

The mindset work by Carol Dweck, and related work specific to math by Jo Boaler, explores the messages about math that we give ourselves and our children that can be helpful or destructive. It can be extremely valuable if every parent and teacher reads at least the book *Mindset: The New Psychology of Success* by Carol Dweck,[1] if not other subsequent books. That book, which most find is an easy and enjoyable read, explores how messages we tell ourselves about who and what we are, and what we can or can't do, impact our abilities a great deal.

For example, did you know that telling children that they are "smart" (or some variation of this) can be counterproductive? As is telling someone, "You are so talented" when they display a work of art or other accomplishment?

Why is this?

Think about what happens if someone says you are good at something that you may or may not be confident about. Let's take as an example finding percentages of something, which you happened to do mentally when at the store with a friend and seeing signs that tell you what percentage off the sale items are.

9

Then imagine you go shopping with the same friend, and this time there is a percentage off that you don't find easy. Maybe last time it was 20% off, and you found that by dividing the price by ten, doubling the amount, and subtracting that from the original price. But this time the percentages are harder, say, 28% off, or you just have exhaustion or brain fog interfering with your thinking.

Even if your friend doesn't openly expect you to perform the mental maneuvers this time, chances are you will feel some kind of pressure to perform the manipulation. If you do, your psychology will determine how you handle that, whether it's by laughing it off, being self-deprecating, secretly calculating it on your phone and pretending you did it mentally, or being embarrassed and working hard to figure out percentages on your own time so you're ready when it comes up again.

This amounts to the feeling of *having something to prove*, which is connected with fear of failure. When people feel like they have a reputation to uphold, it causes stress, which in turn slows down the type of thinking needed to perform the function. There are examples in the *Mindset* book of research that backs this up. For example, students who were told they were smart before a test performed worse than those who weren't told anything.

The messages of *you can't* are also damaging for different reasons. While sometimes they come out verbally, they can be communicated in many other ways. Examples include:

- Grouping struggling students together in consistent groups, not just as needed for specific challenges.
- Tracking in math classes.
- Parent messages of *I hate math* or *I can't do math.*
- Teachers sharing their own struggles or distaste for math.
- Telling students that girls aren't as good at math as boys.
- Calling on one gender more than the other in class.
- The way mistakes are corrected—with undertones of *you are stupid for making that mistake.*

These are all symptoms of *fixed mindset*, or the belief that abilities and aptitudes are inherent. The idea of talent falls into this as well.

The shift here that is so important is toward *growth mindset*, or the understanding that the major differences between success and failure in anything are due to hard work above all.

Yes, some people are born with an easier time than others in some aspects. For example, there are a few genes associated with high athletic accomplishment. However, this isn't predictive; if a child is born with this genetic profile, there's no guarantee they will be a professional athlete. In fact, relying only on innate ability is almost a guarantee of failure.

The *Mindset* book contrasts John McEnroe, who viewed himself as infallible and blamed every failure on external forces—clear symptoms of fixed mindset—with Michael Jordan, who worked endlessly to practice and perfect his basketball skills. If "talent" is what gave McEnroe his success, then nothing would fix it when he started to fail—leading to a shortened career. But with growth mindset, beginning to fail at something is an *opportunity* to work to identify the problem and work to fix it.

That's a key difference: with fixed mindset, problems or mistakes are failures; with growth mindset, they are opportunities.

What challenges did you face in your math education that could be reframed as opportunities?

Another key difference is the understanding that brain growth doesn't stop early in life; the brain continues to grow as new learning happens, and IQ changes over a person's life depending on how they use their mind. This means that learning a musical instrument may be more challenging as an adult, but it's not impossible—along with many other skills and areas of knowledge. The synaptic pruning in early childhood means that the framework may not be there and easy to activate, but with a lot of hard work, it should be possible to develop.

When a person who has worked for years developing their skills as an artist, writer, performer, and the like is told, "You are so talented," that sends the message that it's the talent responsible for the success, not the hard work over years. A person with a talent or aptitude for anything will not go as far as someone with less natural inclination but more hard work.

At the time the Common Core standards were developed, this shift was a major focus. If people believe success is due to talent or intelligence, and they find something challenging, they believe that obviously they aren't intelligent enough for it, so they give up quickly. How many people remember being students and giving up when a math problem was challenging? Teachers, how many students ask for help and expect the answers to be given to them?

The Common Core standards, and most state standards that are derivative of them, contain two sets of standards: the content standards, or *what* we learn, and the practice standards, or *how* we learn it. Most people focus on the content standards; there are many teachers even over ten years after their introduction who have never heard about or been trained on the practice standards! Yet they are at least as important as the content standards. Content can be introduced later; practice can make the difference between wanting to learn or not.

The practice standards are:

1. Make sense of problems and persevere in solving them.
2. Reason abstractly and quantitatively.
3. Construct viable arguments and critique the arguments of others.
4. Model with mathematics.
5. Use appropriate tools strategically.
6. Attend to precision.
7. Look for and make use of structure.
8. Look for and express regularity in repeated reasoning.

These standards, while introduced with the Common Core, remain in some form in most state standards—because they are fundamental to effective math learning and practice. These practices look different at different grade levels and content, but the principles remain the same. We will refer back to them at other times in this book.

THE STORY OF PROBLEM SOLVING

Why did the math textbook sign up for therapy? Because it had so many problems!

The first and arguably most important mathematical practice standard is *Make sense of problems and persevere in solving them.* This sounds simple, but it has many layers. First, the learner needs to understand what the problem is: what is the situation, what's happening within it, and what question is being asked?

This flies in the face of how problem solving, especially word problems, has been taught traditionally, where students have been taught to chop problems into parts. Sometimes this involves excising the information they don't think is relevant to the problem. Sometimes it means going straight for the numbers and circling them, then looking for keywords to try to identify the mathematical operations needed. There are many different stepwise approaches to doing this, but they have one thing in common: they often lead students in the wrong direction.

Instead of chopping up the problem or hyperfocusing on numbers and keywords, this first practice suggests that we *make sense* of problems. Why is this important?

In the first place, consider the reason for word problems. Why, many people wonder, do math programs "cruelly burden" students with complex, multistep word problems?

Since most education situations don't have the facilities, know-how, or time to implement project-based learning, word problems are the closest approximation to putting math into real-life, relevant contexts. Storifying is a powerful technique for communicating many of life's messages and has been used for most of human history to convey messages and information. Therefore, word or story problems are meant to help children make sense of the problems in order to be able to apply math to everyday life challenges.

Unfortunately, that understanding gets lost when educators themselves have had a history of math classes with meaningless or nonsensical word problems. That turns word problems into just another task that has to be completed in math class.

Other issues include publishers that hire low-paid writers without the necessary expertise to create meaningful content, which the author has personally witnessed, and texts that overscaffold the problems. This means that instead of providing a worthy challenge to young minds, the text breaks it down into multiple steps, making the math more accessible but requiring less thinking and therefore promoting less growth. And if the text doesn't do it, the teachers often will do the scaffolding, thinking they are helping the students!

Instead of dissecting the problem, focusing on keywords, or overscaffolding, try these approaches:

- Reframe the problems to be relevant to your students.
- Use student names in the situations.
- Change the situation if needed to be relevant to the children.

For example:

Rafael needed to take the subway three stops to get to school. If he missed his stop and got off two stops too late, then gets on a train going the other direction, how many total extra stops will he have gone through by the time he gets back to school?

This could be a great problem for city-dwelling students. But farm-based students might have trouble envisioning the situation, even if they can do the math. Therefore, the teacher could maintain the educational objective and make it more relevant by rewriting the problem something like this:

Joseph [her student's name] had to ride three miles to school on his bike. He started daydreaming and accidentally rode an extra two miles. After he turned around and got back to school, how many total extra miles did he ride?

The reverse can also be true: rewrite rural situations to be relevant to city-dwelling children.

This can be a lot of extra work for teachers, especially in the first year of a new curriculum. The workload can be lightened by sharing it across grade levels or doing part of it each year and sharing the rewrites year to year.

Alternatively, extra rigor can be provided by asking students to help with this. Ask, "We don't have subways here. What kind of situation can you think of for this story that would make more sense for us?" This can cause the students to connect even more to the situation and make the problem-solving and literacy connection of writing their own problems.

There are a variety of other ways to make complex problem solving achievable in chapter 5.

DEVELOPING MATHEMATICAL UNDERSTANDING

For the first time, I really get it!—Multiple math teachers in professional development sessions

In the previous chapter, we looked at how counting and cardinality develop in early childhood. Building upon this, cardinality continues usually into kindergarten, and then children are ready to work with the numbers they now associate with real-life quantities.

In kindergarten and first grade, children extend the number count to one hundred and beyond. They learn to add and subtract, and they learn about place value.

While none of this is new, it can be overly abstract and meaningless if taught using numerals alone. Even though some students can get very quick and proficient with addition and subtraction facts, this can be more like performing tricks than understanding what's happening.

Why is this important to understand, and how can it transform teaching?

Let's get back into our time machine and travel to when life did not exist on screens and anything you wanted to know wasn't instantaneously available at the push of a button. Even further back, understanding numbers wasn't about school; it was about survival. Are there enough crops? Do we have enough meat? How many hunters or warriors do we have, and how many do the others have? And much more.

If you can picture yourself there, you can imagine how everything was based in the senses. This information was gathered through *experience*.

Even now, although most people's encounters with it are abstract, through words or video, the body of knowledge we have is gathered through experience. For example, data to understand climate change is gathered through hands-on processes. Scientists travel to glaciers to drill ice cores, or deep and long cylinders that have developed over millennia of accumulated ice, like a tree develops rings. The scientists measure the amount of carbon at each layer to understand how our atmosphere has changed, like in Figure 3.1.

Other scientists collect data from ships' logs; for centuries, sailing ships have recorded a variety of data, including sea surface temperature data. These numbers paint a comprehensive picture of the changing sea temperatures. The author's early professional life included a journey to help close some gaps in the data by copying logs from whaling ships at the Mystic Seaport Museum. Other gaps in temperature data were filled in through relationships cultivated by MIT meteorologist Reginald E. Newell, who befriended captains of Japanese illegal whaling ships to obtain the data to fill in areas of the oceans without good data coverage otherwise.

Imagine the senses involved in collecting these data: every hour, no matter what the weather, a captain or crew member would lower a bucket into the ocean to measure the temperature. On sunny days, in torrential rain, in biting wind, the sailors would record the data. The temperature, along with latitude, longitude, time of day, and other data would be handwritten onto a paper log. That log would return and be filed somewhere. Eventually it reached the hands of scientists, who digitized it. That is the story of where sea surface temperature data began.

In current times, the data are collected from a variety of sources, including satellites, buoys, and other measurement devices. But the roots of the data are in human experience.

How does this relate to learning math? Our systems are wired to experience math through the senses so that it is more than abstract knowledge. Not only does this make math more meaningful, but it's a lot more engaging and

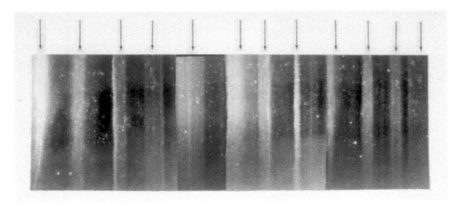

Figure 3.1. An ice core showing lighter summer layers and darker winter layers. *Credit: NOAA (Public domain). https://commons.wikimedia.org/wiki/File:GISP2 _1855m_ice_core_layers.png.*

fun to make math experiential. This is one reason developing the concept is so important.

In the 1990s, the National Council of Teachers of Mathematics recognized this and encouraged a shift toward a conceptual approach to teaching math. This was a step in the right direction and brought manipulatives and constructivist thinking into math classrooms. However, there were shortcomings as well: many teachers didn't understand the concepts themselves, students were left to their own devices to construct the mathematical knowledge of millennia, large numbers were seen as harder than smaller numbers, and more.

Meanwhile, new developments were happening in Singapore. Educators were developing curriculum approaches that integrated conceptual development and traditional algorithms, with an essential intermediate step: pictorial or representational drawings.

This approach brought into action the work of Jerome Bruner. He identified three modes of representation in learning math: "enactive, iconic, and symbolic." Singapore translated this to concrete, pictorial (or representational), and abstract. Bruner stated that these three modes correspond to the development of understanding in children, with each one needing the previous one to appear, and that they all remain mostly intact throughout the person's life.

If we relate this to human development over time, it makes sense. Children start out as concrete thinkers, as humans were for the majority of evolution. Later in evolution, drawing pictures became a way to make transactions more efficient. Whether this was through recording knowledge, understanding, or computations by drawings or writing, or using tally marks to keep track of menstrual cycles, this second stage allowed encoding of concepts on a higher level. Finally, the abstract level developed, allowing humans to use symbols to explore and calculate extreme realms of knowledge: from quantum physics to space exploration, it all begins with math.

Bringing this into the classroom through the concrete, pictorial (or representational), abstract (CPA) approach means that every learner can access the math. Students with learning disabilities tend to struggle to visualize math situations, especially in word problems. Studies show that students with learning challenges are more likely to use overly pictorial and detailed drawings, for example, drawing each flower in a problem with flowers, rather than schematic drawings that show mathematical relationships, which leads to more mistakes.

Using CPA approaches help students, as shown by research, all the way through algebra. Giving students the tools to conceptualize the math, including diagrams to represent unknowns, can support students with learning differences.

In early grades, using objects such as tiles, linking cubes, counting bears, and so forth to represent quantities, and then moving to a more abstract representation of those, will make mental visualization more possible. Eventually the diagrams can be more schematic, with different types for different situations, as will be shown throughout the book.

When designing the Common Core State Standards (CCSS), the authors of the standards identified several interwoven strands that provide the basis for the tapestry of math education. Since most states still use a form of CCSS or derivation of them, it's useful to refer to them here even though they may look a little different in some states. These strands create a big web upon which mathematical understanding is woven. A helpful visual, interactive representation of this can be found on Achieve the Core's coherence map.[2]

In addition to Counting and Cardinality at kindergarten, the strands through grade five are:

- Operations and Algebraic Thinking
- Number and Operations in Base Ten
- Number and Operations—Fractions
- Measurement and Data
- Geometry

Traditionally, these strands have been taught separately. But they aren't separate at all, and the CCSS were written in such a way that they are interconnected and intertwine. A good curriculum will reflect this as well. If a curriculum sticks geometry at the end of each year, where educators are unlikely to reach it, it's probably not a well-designed curriculum.

Once, when the author was training education leaders at the Network Training Institute in Albany, New York, on a fifth-grade chapter that integrated geometry and fraction multiplication, one of the participants reflected, "If I had been taught this way, I would have been able to be an engineer, like I wanted. Instead, I was never able to visualize the math."

What exactly did the presenters do to make this difference? First, every table received large rectangular pieces of construction paper in different sizes that had been planned in advance. Then each table was given square pieces of paper to "tile" the construction paper, meaning that the large rectangles would be covered with nonoverlapping squares, like tiling a floor. The edges of the large papers would have a width that would not equal a whole small square paper, but rather a half or a quarter. The squares could be cut in order to fit everything exactly.

The resulting area could be counted. For example, say you have a tiled rectangle that looks like Figure 3.2.

There are eight whole squares, six half squares, and one quarter square. Adding that together, you get 11¼ square tiles.

This relates to the multiplication of mixed numbers: $4\frac{1}{2} \times 2\frac{1}{2} = 11\frac{1}{4}$. The traditional approach would require changing both mixed numbers into improper fractions and then multiplying, resulting in $\frac{45}{4}$, which when converted back into a mixed number is $11\frac{1}{4}$.

There's nothing wrong at all with that other strategy. It's a great strategy for many math situations. However, teaching with the rectangles has these advantages:

- It demonstrates the concept of what we are doing when we find area— we are finding how many squares of a unit cover an object. This has many real-life applications, including buying flooring.
- It provides an experiential link for the area model for multiplication, an excellent model that can be used to simplify complex computations.
- It provides a concrete connection to fractions and their relationships, with cutting the paper and adding the fractional parts together.
- There are fewer computational steps with opportunities for errors presented in the improper fraction strategy.
- It provides a foundation for practicing the *distributive property* to multiply *polynomials* in middle and high school.
- It provides another strategy to check one's work.

Also note that this activity integrates geometry (finding area of a rectangle), operations with fractions, and measurement. And this is only one conceptual activity! Imagine a whole learning career with this type of approach. There are plenty more strategies and approaches on this in chapter 7.

For younger students, counting and sequencing can be made more engaging by integrating math with movement. Suzy Koontz has ideas and training programs for this.[3] You can also find "fraction jacks," an activity created by the author, on the author's website.[4]

In addition, there is some guidance for this in the movement sections of mathematical Sprints, a fluency practice designed by Yoram Sagher and made available widely through Eureka Math. You can find a clickable compilation of Sprints linked to the author's website, as well as a description of how to implement a Sprint, including movement. Students enjoy the high-energy aspects of these, as well as the competition with themselves to do better.

PLACE VALUE: A KEY UNDERSTANDING

One of the biggest challenges in learning math is language, which has an important place in mathematical development from an early age. In the

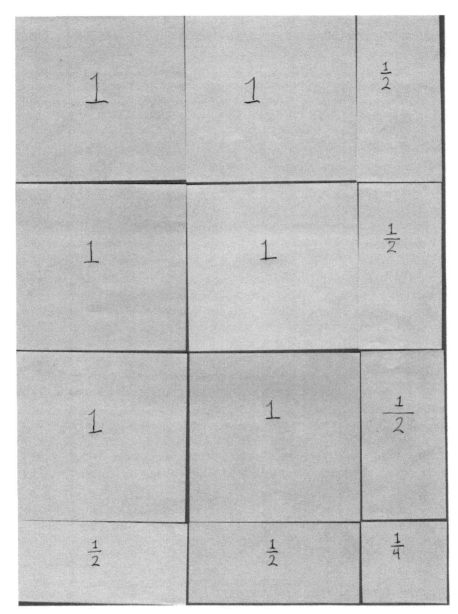

Figure 3.2. A rectangular piece of paper tiled with square units.

"Infancy" and "Early Childhood" chapters, we saw how language development provides a foundation for understanding counting sequences. This also appears with place value understanding.

In some languages, including Mandarin, the pattern of counting is based on place value. The count goes one to ten, and then the next decade is counted like this: ten-one, ten-two, ten-three, and so on. When twenty is reached, the number is said "two-ten." This matches how we write numbers using place value exactly and supports early understanding of numerals in base ten. This structure is in stark contrast to English and some other Latin-based languages, where in the teens, the numbers have no resemblance whatsoever to place value.

Think about it. *Eleven*? *Twelve*?! How do those make sense to a young life trying to make sense of numbers? They are so different that culturally, English speakers have created a special category of children we call "preteen" or "tweens." Many children don't feel like they have entered their teens officially unless they are in a year that ends in "-teen"! While this may have a connection with puberty, it also sets a language-based boundary that is somewhat arbitrary, as puberty can develop anywhere from age nine to sixteen.

Did you know that the origin of "eleven" is "one left," or one more than ten, and of "twelve" is "two left"? Even in the later teen numbers, where there are some patterns that resemble the counting numbers, the ten or "-teen" comes after the number in the ones place, which is the opposite of how they are written. "Fifteen" is written one-five, or the one ten followed by the five. This explains why many children reverse their digits when learning to write numbers between ten and twenty.

To address this issue, one approach is called "Say Ten counting." This is a way to count in English that mirrors the Mandarin structure. So instead of counting one, two, three . . . ten, eleven, twelve, you would count one, two, three . . . ten, ten-one, ten-two, ten-three, and so on. Once you reach twenty, it's "two-ten, two-ten-one, two-ten-two," and so on.

It's important to introduce this way of counting after children are fluent in the regular English sequence so they can make the connections; counting both ways, and translating back and forth with visuals of tens and ones in objects, will reinforce the children's ability to count and connect to the cardinality.

How might this look? Imagine a kindergarten teacher with a group of students, or even one student. Both the teacher and the students, if possible, have their own rekenrek. If that isn't possible, the teacher models the activity using a virtual rekenrek such as a number rack by the Math Learning Center,[5] which can be projected on an interactive whiteboard. Only two or three lines of beads should be shown, like in the rekenrek in Figure 3.3.

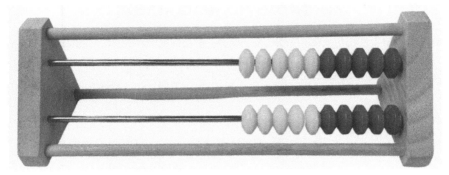

Figure 3.3.   An example of a rekenrek.

Then the teacher and the students count together while moving beads from right to left, counting, "One, two, three," and so on. This reinforces cardinality at the same time. The standard count continues to twenty.

Next, the beads are reset and the counting begins again, only this time, after filling a row of ten beads, the next row starts with "ten-one" and continues until two-ten. Two rows of ten beads are now filled.

This is a good place to stop and discuss when introducing the activity. Questions can include:

- What were we doing in this activity?
- What was the same about our counting both ways?
- What was different in how we counted both ways?
- What connections can you make between the beads and the Say Ten counting way?

In the classroom, these questions can be discussed in partners or groups, and then the teacher can facilitate a whole-group discussion.

As the children develop understanding and comfort with this new skill, additional complexities can be added. Counting backward using both methods of counting while removing beads is an important one. After the first few times of counting with the rekenrek a new way, students can have the option of using it or counting without it, as the goal is visualization. Counting up to thirty and eventually forty can be developed in time.

Say Ten counting should continue through second grade, as students develop and add onto their understanding of place value. It can be useful when working with hundreds and thousands as well.

ADDITION AND SUBTRACTION

One of the key questions that can cause a revelation in the understanding about math is, "What is number sense?" Consider taking a moment to try to define this for yourself and writing your thoughts here:

Did you come up with something like, "The ability to compose and decompose numbers"?

Let's explore this a bit. The earliest understanding of numbers is the number count. Later, children relate quantities to the number names. Eventually, they start to learn to put numbers together and take them apart.

If their only exposure to the last is by "facts" on worksheets or flash cards, then most likely some students with better recall ability will come out feeling "good at math," while others will struggle and begin the journey of feeling like they don't understand math, leading to dislike of the subject and possible math phobia.

A key to avoiding these pitfalls is a focus on *part-whole understanding*. The basis of this is the key understanding that every number (whole number, in this case) is a sum of ones. We know this, but are the connections made when helping students to understand addition and subtraction?

In the author's experience as a math coach, looking at numbers this way can be a revelation even to seasoned math teachers, because they were taught numbers as distinct, unconnected entities. For example, in the unconnected way of thinking, three is just three; it's not $1 + 1 + 1$, or $2 + 1$, or $1 + 2$, or $3 + 0$, or $0 + 3$. However, a thinker who learns with part-whole understanding does look at numbers that way.

Once this understanding is solid, working with place value can extend it to manipulating larger numbers. If we know $1 + 2 = 3$, then one *ten* plus two *tens* equals three *tens*, or $10 + 20 = 30$. Therefore, $100 + 200 = 300$, $0.1 + 0.2 = 0.3$, and so forth. And as is explored in chapter 7, learning fractions as countable units allows easy addition and subtraction as well: one-fourth plus two-fourths equals three-fourths, for instance.

Other models besides the rekenrek to help develop addition and subtraction are number bonds and part-whole diagrams.

Frequent use of these will help students grasp the fact that parts go together to make a whole (addition), and we decompose a whole to find parts (subtraction). If students struggle with these operations, using the

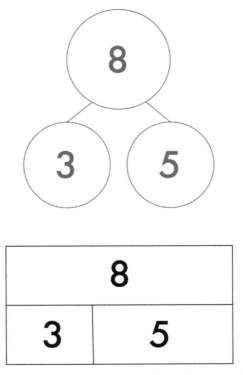

Figure 3.4.   A number bond and part-whole model showing numerical relationships.

models—starting with manipulatives, moving to drawings, and finally using numbers—can help.

MULTIPLICATION AND DIVISION

When is the best time to introduce multiplication and division? Given the fact that so many students struggle to know their tables, which impacts later learning, many educators and parents push them younger and younger. However, is learning them by rote the most effective way to learn them?

Let's step backward for a minute and think in a connected way again. Where did multiplication and division come from, and why do we use these operations?

Let's try traveling back in time before schooling was common. Imagine being the head of a family that grows and farms at least some of your own food, including chickens. You know that each member of the family needs two eggs per day for breakfast. How would you know how many to keep for your family and how many would be left over to sell or store? If there are five members of your family, you could count by ones, mentally distributing an egg to each member: one, two, three, four, five, and starting again, six, seven, eight, nine, ten. Okay, anything over ten eggs per day per day can be sold or saved for later.

If you can count by twos, this process becomes faster: counting eggs is two, four, six, eight, ten. If you can count by fives, it's faster still: two for each person is five, ten. This leads to two fives is ten, or $2 \times 5 = 10$ or five twos is ten, or $5 \times 2 = 10^6$ Using multiplication makes it more efficient to keep track.

What about division? We can stay with the hens and eggs with this. Let's say this day, the hens laid thirteen eggs. We can mentally distribute the eggs to the family members, keeping track with our fingers, or if we prefer, we can put the eggs onto plates, or draw a diagram with five empty circles and draw dots to represent each egg. Then using our chosen method, we can distribute the eggs to each person until each has two: one, two, three, four, five, six, seven, eight, nine, ten.

Then we have three left over to sell or store—our remainder.

Again, if we know how to divide, we know that we need to have at least ten eggs for each person to get two eggs. Since thirteen is more than ten, we know that we can set three aside, and then we can divide the ten among five people to get two each. Another way to look at is to divide the thirteen into

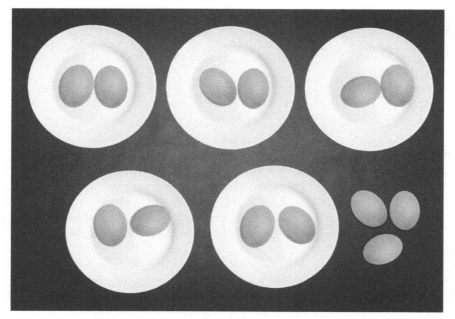

Figure 3.5. Visual model of dividing thirteen by five using eggs and plates.

groups of two. This gives six groups with one egg left over. The extra group of two and the extra egg can be combined to sell or save.

What real-life situations can you and your student(s) relate to these examples?

Current thinking suggests that developing the foundations for multiplication is more important in early years, particularly in countries where students start elementary school around age six. Countries where students start a year or so later have a different developmental age to work with, which many laypeople don't take into account when comparing results and curricula from different countries.

This means that rather than memorizing or learning tables, students can lay a foundation for understanding the patterns in a few different ways:

- Skip-counting in different patterns, like twos, tens, and fives, in kindergarten and first grade, can be fun and introduce pattern recognition.
- Skip-counting in second grade with threes and fours can add to the repertoire. It's helpful at this point to include counting backward. A good way to introduce fours is to introduce twos with whisper-counting every other count. This would look like the following, where italics indicate whispered numbers:
  - Zero, *two*, four, *six*, eight, *ten*, twelve, *fourteen*, sixteen, and so on. Students would pay attention to the louder numbers to learn and practice counting by fours.
- Working with small groupings of objects and arrays in grade two can lead to the understanding of repeated addition underlying multiplication. For example, if a child builds an array of tiles with three rows of five tiles, they can count across $(3 + 3 + 3 + 3 + 3 = 15)$ or down $(5 + 5 + 5 = 15)$.

How does this build into success in multiplication and division?

This is a process of understanding patterns, rather than memorizing by rote. This is important because there are so many students who find memorizing difficult. Providing a variety of access points to learning these facts is a key to success for all learners.

Later, in third grade, they can connect this to how many *times* they added the number: "I added three five times, so five times the number three is 15. I added five three times, so three times the number five is 15. Hey, it's the same numbers in the opposite order!"

IMPORTANT PRACTICES

- Reframe problems as opportunities.
- Enjoy the process of mistakes as ways to learn.
- Encourage children to focus on the process of learning math.
- If you had a negative childhood math experience, see it as an opportunity to learn as an adult rather than communicating negativity to children.
- Embrace problem solving as a way to function better in life.
- Reframe math problems in contexts that are relevant to your children.
- When introducing a new math concept, find ways to do it with hands-on tools, then moving to a pictorial representation, and finally abstract computation.
- Involve movement in counting and fluency practice.
- Try Say Ten counting activities.

What about your elementary schooling do you think would have been improved through any of the approaches in this chapter?

The author wonders how much better off world economies would be if foundational math knowledge were meaningful and universal.

NOTES

1. Carol S. Dweck, *Mindset: The New Psychology of Success: How We Can Learn to Fulfill Our Potential* (New York: Random House, 2006).

2. The coherence map can be found at achievethecore.org/coherence-map/.

3. Her resources are available at mathandmovement.com/.

4. Find the activity at susanmidlarsky.com/fraction-jacks-or-if-youre-british -fraction-stars/.

5. Find the number rack and other free online manipulatives at www .mathlearningcenter.org/apps/.

6. For the sake of this book, the first factor will be the number of terms, and the second will be the quantity we are multiplying.

Chapter 4

Interlude 1

Why Does Math Exist?

As above, so below.

Every math teacher has heard, "Why do we have to learn this?" about whatever they are teaching at the moment. This happens more and more as students get older, as learning changes from a joy into a chore in many students' minds.

There are so many easy answers to this in our daily adult lives. Unfortunately, they tend to be dry and not very much fun. Not too many children are excited by the answer, "So you can do your own taxes," for example.

To delve deeper into this, let's step into a time machine and travel to a time before computers, cars, cell phones, refrigerators—all the trappings of our modern lives.

From the earliest times, humans developed counting to keep track of things: Are all our children home safe? How many days have passed since the last menstrual cycle? When will the bad weather be coming? Is there enough food? They watched the skies and the plants and animals on the ground and gradually developed systems to understand how things worked. Many of these became encapsulated in wisdom stories passed down through generations. Other cultures took it to paintings, like in cave paintings, or to symbolism, like in ancient Egypt.

Eventually, humans developed more sophisticated number systems. These allowed for construction of buildings that were structurally sound, agricultural planning, road systems, water storage, and much more. They also opened the world of how to understand the movement of the stars, the planets, and our own planet.

Now mathematics is found in every field. It can be fun to challenge students to name a job or career that they think won't require math. Then tell them how math is involved. Before long, other students will provide ideas about this too. The goal is for them to ultimately conclude for themselves that math is in everything.

Some examples that have come out of conversations with students are:

- Art—Proportion, geometry, scaling
- Sports—Geometry (of shots/goals), timing, physics
- Retail—Being able to reconcile a register, accounting for inventory
- Food production—Proportions of ingredients, ordering, anticipating customer levels, and so forth
- Dancing—Choreography to music, position, timing, patterns and relationships, exercise time for strength without injury
- Fashion design—Geometry and measurement, calculating amount of fabric needed, costs, time to create fashions

There are more ideas and examples in chapter 8.

One story that math-resistant high school students enjoy is the story of a carpenter who had dropped out of high school at sixteen. He was building an attic and was trying to predict how much wood he needed for the slanted roof. He knew the height and width, but he couldn't figure out the length of the slanted side. At the time, while the author hadn't been in school for years and wasn't on the path of being a teacher yet, her long-term memory dredged up the Pythagorean theorem. This helped him calculate the measurements. He stared at the author in wonder and said, "If I knew they taught useful stuff in high school, I would have stayed."

But if he hadn't been taught the Pythagorean theorem in a way that made it relevant, it still might not have helped him with his problem.

There hasn't been a class that has stumped the author yet in finding examples of needing math in life! Often the students realize that the simple fact of needing to understand and deal with adult finances is enough to make math valuable.

Even more, understanding numbers and math allows us to perceive systems and patterns. We improve our grasp of how things work in ourselves, in our lives, and between all things. This is because the same natural laws govern everything in the universe. And that's why astrophysicists can study the farthest reaches of the universe without being able to see or travel there, along with scientists who study the smallest possible forces and particles of matter. The laws of nature and physics govern everything, and mathematics is one entry into this understanding.

Returning to Earth, some thought-provoking questions that could be productively explored in a Socratic seminar or other student-focused discussion are: What are numbers? Where do they come from?

After reflecting on this, the reader might come to the realization that numbers are ways humans represent quantities and patterns that exist all around us. A deeper study can cause one to fall in love with numbers.

How can this happen? If we put down our devices and start to look carefully at nature and how things work, new understandings can be revealed. Below are some examples from the author's own experience; students who embark on a journey of curiosity about these become fascinated and enriched. They are only minor starting points with ideas to get you and your students started on your own journeys.

These examples, along with tips for multiplying or dividing by the number, are starting points for you to build upon and find more examples that show the patterns, or to try to disprove. We'll start with two, as this is easy to see.

Two (2): Look at our own bodies. How many limbs of each kind do humans generally have? Yes, two! Everything on the outside (though not the inside) seems balanced, with apparent bilateral symmetry.

Now look around and see other places where duality exists in nature. Pretty much every leaf is divided in two; animals have two halves; we have two types of light-sensing equipment in our eyes, rods and cones; there are odd and even numbers; and on and on. Try to draw *anything* without lines and/ or curves!

There is a fancy name for this—dualism—and philosophers such as Emerson wrote volumes exploring it. It is just one of the many patterns in nature.

What about the patterns in computation? Have you noticed that all whole numbers multiplied by two are even, and all even numbers are divisible by two? Mentally, we can use doubling and halving.

When adding or subtracting, if we start with an even number and add two, we get another even number. If we start with an odd number, we end with an odd number.

Returning to one (1): almost no examples are easy to find, except that each one of us is completely unique, with different fingerprints from everyone else. There is also only one Earth.

To multiply or divide by one means the number we're using comes out the same on the other side. Adding or subtracting one means the value changes by one; all whole numbers are sums of one.

If we want to use mathematical language for this, we can speak of the *identity property of multiplication*, which is that any number multiplied by one ends up with itself again—for example, $712 \times 1 = 712$.

Compare and contrast this with the number nine, when we get to it.

Three (3): Here we can see stability, especially in matter and organic life. The three parts of an atom, the three elements in organic life (carbon, oxygen, hydrogen), the three celestial bodies that impact our lives the most (sun, planet, moon).

The pattern of multiplying by three alternates odd and even products (3, 6, 9, 12, etc.). To see if a number is divisible by three, add its digits to see if the sum is divisible by three. If it is, the number is divisible by three. For example, take 231. Its digits are 2, 3, and 1. Add them together: $2 + 3 + 1 = 6$. Since the sum, six, is divisible by three, the number is divisible by three.

Four (4): A number associated with cycles, such as the seasons, or the four reproductive cycles of a woman. In a group of four people, one person will usually be excluded; watch this and see for yourself.

To multiply by four, double the number and then double it again. To see if it's divisible, cut the number in half. If the result is even, the number is divisible by four. Cut it in half again to get the quotient, or the answer to the division problem.

Five (5): This number bears fruit—literally! Nearly all fruit-producing plants have flowers with five petals, while those with three or six make pods. Cutting an apple in half vertically shows a five-pointed star inside, which is formed from the original structure of the flower; similar structures can be found in other fruits developed from five petals. We have five fingers on each hand and can make a five-pointed star when our limbs are outstretched.

Multiples of five have a zero or five in the ones place. To multiply by five, either count by fives and track which multiple you are on, or multiply by ten (append a zero) and cut the result in half. Examples:

- Count by fives to get 5×8: 5, 10, 15, 20, 25, 30, 35, 40.
- Multiply by ten and cut in half: $10 \times 8 = 80$, and half of 80 is 40.

Six (6): Creatures with six legs wear their skeletons on the outside. It seems to be a number of double stability, like with two interlocking triangles.

Since six is a composite number with three and two as its factors, we can use the three and two rules combined to multiply. Multiples of six are multiples of three, then doubled. For example, $3 \times 5 = 15$. Therefore, $6 \times 5 = 15 \times 2$ (15 doubled), or 30.

We can use the converse to divide, meaning we can divide by three and then two or two and then three, whichever is easiest. Checking for divisibility is the same as the three rule, but the original number must also be even. For example, adding the digits in 123 gives us $1 + 2 + 3 = 6$, but since 123 isn't even, the number is divisible by three and *not* six. However, 132 is even, and $1 + 3 + 2 = 6$, so the same digits as 123 but in a different order have a different outcome. This number is divisible by six.

Seven (7): Long considered a lucky number, seven is found in so many places around us, including seven holes in our heads. (Did you know there are seven holes in our heads?) Why is there such a fascination with this number? It's the hardest of the base numbers to multiply or divide mentally, too. Why?

To mentally multiply by seven, it may be easiest to multiply by six and add one more set of the other factor on. For example, $7 \times 12 = (6 \times 12) + (1 \times 12) = 72 + 12 = 84$. This uses the distributive property and decomposing, explored in chapter 3 in the section on multiplication strategies, so it isn't unique to sevens but can be used for them.

To see if a number is divisible by seven, double the ones digit and subtract the result from the rest of the digits, treating their place value as though the ones place didn't exist. For example, take 154. Double the four ($4 \times 2 = 8$) and subtract that from the other digits, or 15. $15 - 8 = 7$, so the number is divisible by seven.

While there may not be easy ways to divide mentally by seven, there is a great pattern when it comes to fractions with denominator seven. The decimal equivalent to 17 is 0.142857, repeating. A way to recall this is $7 \times 2 = 14$, 7 $\times 4 = 28$, and $7 \times 8 = 56$; add one to the last and you get 57. What an amazing pattern!

Eight (8): This is found in doubles of fours, like in the legs of an arachnid. Also as with sixes, it seems to come with a harder "shell" than the other numbers.

For multiplying, think about eight as two to the third power, or $2 \times 2 \times 2$. Thus to multiply by eight, just double, double, and double again.

To check if a number is divisible by eight, use the four rule twice. Cut the number in half: Is it even? If so, divide it in two again. If it's still even, it's divisible by eight. Complete the last division step to find the quotient.

Nine (9): This is hard to find natural examples for here on Earth and has led to mysticism surrounding the Enneagram. However, we can find a few examples. Nine months of human pregnancy; nine planets in our solar system until Pluto was disqualified; nine counting numbers in the decimal system.

Nine gets really interesting when we compute with it. The system of finding a root number, meaning the sum of all digits in a number until you get to one digit, erases the value of the nine. For example, 1973: $1 + 9 + 7 + 3 = 10 + 10 = 20$. $2 + 0 = 2$. Take out the nine, and you get the same value: $1 + 7 + 3 = 1 + 10 = 11$; $1 + 1 = 2$.[1]

Conversely, multiplying by nine turns every other number into a root of nine. For example: $8 \times 9 = 72$. $7 + 2 = 9$. Look at the pattern of the nines table: 9, 18, 27, 36, and so on. Every multiple of nine has its digits sum or root to nine. This is one reason nine is called the magic number.

Our hands have a special relationship to nine as well. How is this, with ten fingers? Well, try this. To multiply 5×9, put both hands in front of you, facing the backs of your hands, with fingers extended. Beginning from the left pinky, count, "One, two, three, four, five." (Some people move the finger they are counting when they do this.) Then fold the fifth finger, your left thumb, into your palm. The remaining straight fingers make the product: the fingers to the left (four) make the tens place, and the fingers to the right of the folded digits (five) make the ones place: 45.

Try it again, using 7×9. Count along from the left to the right until you get to seven, That should bring you to the right index finger; fold that down. How many to the left? Six. How many to the right? Three. The product is 63.

We can use this for division as well. First we use divisibility pattern we discovered before: any product of nine has to have its digits sum to nine. If it's a two-digit number whose digits sum to nine, we can divide it using our hands.

Take the number 72. Represent it using your hands. You will need seven digits to the left of the folded finger; this means your right middle finger will fold. That leaves two to the right, representing the two in the ones place.

This time we count to find out the quotient of $72 \div 9$. Counting our fingers until we get to the folded finger, we find it's the eighth finger, so the quotient is eight.

What is the relationship between nine and ten that makes this computation strategy possible?

Zero (0): A late appearance on the number scene, this symbol represents *nothing* or absence, which doesn't exist in our daily life except in the abstract. However, without it, we would not be able to have our decimal number system or place value. In addition, it gives us the *identity property of addition*, which is that when you add any number to zero, you get the original number back. We can add, subtract, and multiply with zero, but division only goes one way—we can divide zero, but we can't divide by it. Do you know why this is?

Researching the history and properties of this digit can be fascinating to do with your students!

What are some examples of these numbers you can find? And what other patterns can you find? What do you wonder about them?
The author wonders what the different patterns point to.

NOTE

1. Note that the addition here makes use of the "make-a-ten" strategy, meaning instead of adding the numbers in order, we use the *commutative property* to find tens and use those to make the addition easier.

Chapter 5

Problem Solving, or Equipping Students for Life

Mathematics may not teach us to add love or subtract hate, but it gives us hope that every problem has a solution.—Anonymous

As we saw in chapter 3, problem solving is often met with resistance in math class. When students get stuck on challenging questions, they often seek "help" in the form of answers instead of persevering to find them on their own. Teachers commonly provide answers instead of guiding students onto pathways of discovery for themselves. Even when teachers ask students to help each other, unless the students have been shown other ways, the students will often tell each other the solutions.

Let's translate this into adult life. What happens when a mind that's been trained in this way confronts a sticky problem, for example, a car breakdown on a highway when on the way to a job interview?

While it's natural to panic a bit in this situation, a person who has not developed problem-solving skills will most likely reach out to an authority for "help," or being saved. They may call a parent or a mechanic or a roadside service company as a first move. Or if very dependent, they may stay frozen and possibly overwhelmed or crying in the car, unsure of what to do at all.

On the other hand, a person who has developed these skills is more likely, after the initial panic, to calm down and utilize their problem-solving skills. They may contact the job interviewer first to let them know about the situation. Then they may look to assess what the problem is before acting. They will make sure that the vehicle is in a safe enough location and use safety indicators like flashers or flares to prevent harm. If it's within their scope to remedy, they may attempt to solve the problem themselves; otherwise, they will contact the appropriate party. Then they will try to reschedule the interview if necessary.

A person with strong problem-solving skills is able to navigate the rocky roads of life more capably than one who is always given the answers by an authority. In fact, a very good math teacher will make it so the students almost never look to the teacher for the answers; instead, the students are equipped with the skills to discover the answers and find out if they are correct themselves. The teacher is there to facilitate the development of these skills, not to be the all-knowing presence in the classroom.

This translates into a term that is often heard in classrooms these days, *productive struggle*. This type of struggle lands in the zone of proximal development (ZPD), a term coined by Lev Vygotsky, which is the gap between too easy and too hard. It leads to students developing perseverance. In essence, this theory says that there is a level at which we can do a task easily, which can make it boring; a level at which things are too hard or challenging, which can lead to frustration; and a level at which the challenge is exciting but achievable, which is appropriate for growth.

With a history of an academic pathway in schools that provides little preparation for real life, where the answer to questions is, "Because I told you so," traditional learning leads to adults with less critical thinking than is ideal for those who seek to make a mark on life. If you want stronger problem-solving skills for your students, altering the education style at this point and offering lots of problem-solving opportunities is a good place to start.

What are some situations in your life you can relate to this process? When were you stuck, and when were you able to successfully solve the problem? What made the difference?

VISUALIZATION STRATEGIES
FOR PROBLEM SOLVING

In chapter 3, we learned about the concrete-pictorial-abstract approach to learning math concepts, identified and implemented with great success in Singapore, then spreading to the rest of the world. A huge breakthrough, particularly in problem solving, was the development of the bar model (also known as bar diagram or tape diagram). Here is an example of a math problem from a fourth-grade level. Why don't you try to solve it before reading the solution?

Marnie and Pete have 48 pennies together. After Marnie gives Pete 12 pennies, she has twice as many pennies as Pete. How many pennies did Marnie start off with?

Give this a try! Then come back and compare your approach to what is shown here.

In the classroom, or in homeschool, it's a good idea to allow students to use what tools they have and strategies they know to try to solve this. For example, you might have coins the child can use to work out the problem. If not, any countable item, like dried beans or marbles, can be used.

If you're like most people, this problem might be a little challenging. But this is the kind of challenge fourth graders are expected to meet. Maybe now it's more obvious why some teachers overscaffold!

Let's look at how the bar modeling from Singapore helps to break this down. This is a "before-and-after" problem, meaning there is a situation at the beginning and a situation at the end, with a change in the middle. What we are left with is a question about the beginning, or "start unknown."

While this way is not the only approach, here is one way to think about this:

If Marnie ends up with twice as many pennies as Pete after giving some to him, she started off with more than twice as many pennies as Pete. So draw two bars, like in Figure 5.1, with one at least more than twice as long as the other. One is drawn above the other because it's a comparison problem, so seeing the lengths measured against each other makes it easier to compare. One bracket shows the total of 48 pennies, and one with a question mark shows the unknown we are trying to identify.

Then show 12 moving from Marnie's to Pete's, like in Figure 5.2. This also shows that Marnie's is now worth two of Pete's by length measurement.

Thus 12 plus some quantity is half of Marnie's, and the whole thing equals 48. There are three equal bars, so divide 48 by 3 to know that each individual bar has to equal 16.

Therefore, since Marnie's new total bar consists of 2 smaller bars, that means her new number of pennies is 2 × 16, or 32. Add the 12 from before to find her original quantity, and Marnie had 44 pennies originally!

Number of Pennies

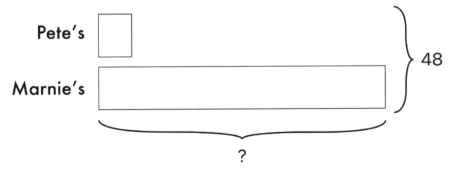

Figure 5.1. The comparison bar model as the situation begins.

Number of Pennies

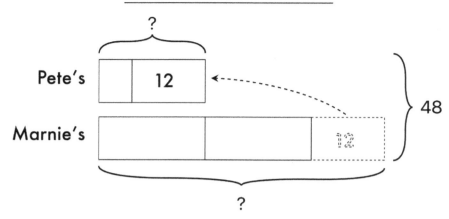

Figure 5.2.   The model as 12 pennies are given to Pete.

To check this, we can write the numbers back into the model and see if it all works, like in Figure 5.3.

What did you think? Did you follow this? If not, try drawing it out yourself to experience the process.

This is just one example to show how illustrations can help. There are many simpler examples, as well as more complex ones; in practice, beginning with a slightly complex example that might challenge adults to show how the modeling can simplify the problem solving can help prove the point.

To practice model drawing for problem solving, a good online tool is Thinking Blocks on Math Playground.[1] After learning how they work and practicing with the digital tools, it's a good idea for students to learn how to draw the models. Eureka Math,[2] available for free, has many excellent examples of how this looks at multiple grade levels and mathematical topics.

OPEN-ENDED PROBLEM SOLVING

The goal of mathematical problem solving in so many people's minds is what? The answer! This leads to a false certainty about life, and potentially black-and-white thinking. Many people say they enjoy math because there is a "right answer." In some ways, in a confusing and uncertain world, this can be understandable.

But let's think about real-world applications in math. Perhaps you are working for a space agency and want to calculate a time and trajectory for launching a satellite. There are many factors involved, and there is usually

Number of Pennies

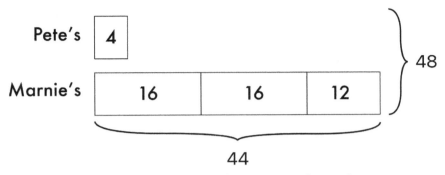

Figure 5.3.   **The original situation with numbers to answer the question.**

an ideal window, not an ideal instant in time. If that window is missed due to weather or malfunction, another window may take a long time to appear, but it will appear.

Always trying to get "the right answer" leads to oversimplification and looking to authority for validation and correction. This can be anxiety producing as well, because what if you are wrong? How will that wrong answer be dealt with?

In life, there usually isn't just one right answer. Even if there is, it often doesn't matter very much. For example, there is one right answer to the question, "How many stripes are there on the American flag?" If one doesn't know the answer, it's easy to look up. What is more important is the *why* behind those stripes.

When students are encouraged to step outside certainty, they are more likely to take risks. Taking risks and being successful at least some of the time is a great way for students to develop confidence and perseverance.

What if we took the focus off right answers in math class and moved it toward the *process* of problem solving?

To do this, we can open up problems in two ways:

- Multiple processes or strategies to find solutions
- Problems with more than one right answer

In the first instance, we move away from teaching students *one strategy or path to finding a solution* toward *many strategies or paths*. When observing a math class where students are solving problems, it's important to see how students are solving the problems.

For example, let's say fourth graders are adding $\frac{3}{4}$ and $\frac{2}{5}$. In some classes, every single student will find common denominators by multiplying the first fraction by $\frac{5}{5}$ and the second by $\frac{4}{4}$, and then adding $\frac{15}{20} + \frac{8}{20}$ to find $\frac{23}{20}$, and finally dividing to make the mixed number $1\frac{3}{20}$, which is a common procedural approach.

Traditionally in this case, the teacher would be regarded as a good teacher because all the students are able to successfully solve the addition equation. However, if you ask one or more students why they are using this approach, most of them will only be able to say it's because that's how you do it, or because you have to make common denominators, or because that's how they were taught. They are missing the conceptual underpinnings.

If some students are using manipulatives and others are using fraction models or number lines, then you are much more likely to find multiple students who can explain what it means to find common denominators and why we should do it.

If the concepts are taught *after* the students learn the procedures, the students usually resist learning the concepts because it's more work to think more deeply. They don't want to be bothered. Teachers often don't want to be bothered either!

However, when we teach the procedure only, without the conceptual underpinning, we are much more likely to see common errors such as failing to convert to common units and just adding across. In this case it would be $\frac{3}{4} + \frac{2}{5} = \frac{5}{9}$, which is not true. Procedural teaching engages working memory, not deeper long-term memory. So procedural teaching seems to save time and work, but it requires more effort in the long term. There is a lot more on working with fractions in chapter 7.

How do we engage students in multiple approaches for problem solving? One way to do so is to engage students in discussing solution strategies often. For example, let's say second-grade students are given the problem 48 + 63 to solve mentally. After finding the solution—and in this case there is only one—students discuss how they solved it. Here is an example of how this might sound.

Teacher: Joseph, how did you find your answer?

Joseph: I added the tens, so 40 and 60, and that made 100, and I kept that in my head. Then I added 8 and 3, and that made 11, so I added that to 100 in my head, so 111.

Teacher: Raise your hand if you did it the same way. Okay, four other students. Who did it a different way? Aleah?

Aleah: I added the 8 and the 3 first. Then I added the 10 in the 11 to the 40, so I made it 50, and added that to 60. I thought 5 and 6 is 11, so 5 tens and 6 tens is 11 tens, so 110, and then I added the 1 in 11 to 110, so 111.

Teacher: How many other students did it this way? Five? Great!

To extend this, especially if the solution strategies are limited and time allows, add an even more open-ended approach:

Teacher: And what is a way we haven't thought of yet?

Students can work on this individually or in groups, and then share.

Not only does this allow students to learn different ways of thinking about math and numbers from their peers, it also validates their thinking and helps students learn to communicate their thinking. This creates deeper neurological pathways for the math connections to grow.

In this situation, while there is one numerical right answer, there are many different "right answers" for how the students get there. Moving away from multiple choice into written responses means the thinking can be more transparent, allowing teachers to support student learning and identify gaps and common misconceptions.

Additionally, some curricula, even newer ones, step out the problems in a scaffolded way as a model for problem solving. While this might be helpful for some students with diagnosed learning differences, it defeats the purpose of rigorous problem solving because

- students are directed toward certain "steps" to solving a problem;
- this leads to thinking there is only one right approach to problem solving; and
- it takes away the opportunities for productive struggle.

How does it look to have math problems that have more than one right answer?

There are many ways these can be presented. Below are some examples of problems and some sample student responses.

At the earliest level, it might look like _____ + _____ = 7, allowing students to choose which addends they want to use.

> *Student response 1:* $0 + 7 = 7$
> *Student response 2:* $2 + 5 = 7$

Or there might be a number bond that looks like the one in Figure 5.4.

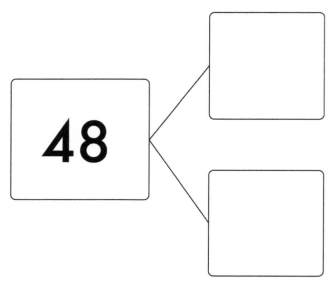

Figure 5.4.   An open-ended number bond with a whole of 48.

In this case, the challenge could be, "Write a word problem with your own numbers that goes with this number bond."

Student response 1: There were 40 apples in one basket and 8 in the other. How many apples were there altogether?

Student response 2: One group had 32 apples. The other had 16. How many apples did they have together?

In geometry, it could be, "Create a quadrilateral that has four equal sides. Name the quadrilateral, and explain why it is the name you gave."

Student response 1: I made a square because all four sides are equal plus all the angles are right angles.

Student response 2: I made a rhombus because all four sides are the same but the angles aren't right angles.

Students could be given a fraction, say, $5/12$, and given the challenge, "Make two different multiplication equations with the product $\frac{1}{2}$, and show they are correct by writing or drawing."

Student response 1: $5/4 \times 2/5$ because $5 \times 2 = 10$ and $4 \times 5 = 20$, and $10/20$ is the same as $\frac{1}{2}$. And then $1/3 \times 3/2$, because $1 \times 3 = 3$ and $3 \times 2 = 6$, and $3/6 = \frac{1}{2}$.

Student response 2: $2/3 \times 3/4 = 6/12 = \frac{1}{2}$ [with drawing] and $1/7 \times 7/2 = \frac{1}{2}$ [also with drawing; see Figure 5.5]

Each of these reveals a lot about the student's thinking about multiplying fractions.

Other possibilities include showing a pattern and asking students to write an equation to match the pattern, like in Figure 5.6.[3] For example, "How do you see the shapes changing?" The students could respond in different ways.

Student response 1: I see one added on each side and one added on the top of the middle ones each time.

Student response 2: I see the center one growing, and like steps, the ones on the side are following the middle one.

Another type of open-ended problem is reversing the standard approach to word problems. In this case, there could be a sentence that is the answer to a word problem, and the students have to write their own problem to match it—similar to the structure of a "math problem *Jeopardy*," except with multiple right answers and no speed or competition required. For example, "Answer: There are 18 students on the school bus."

Student question 1: The bus picks up 9 students at one stop, 7 students at the next stop, and 2 students at the third stop. How many students are on the bus now?

Student question 2: The bus picks up 35 students from school to drop them off. It drops off 17 students in the first 15 minutes. How many students are left on the bus?

Student question 3: The bus picks up 3 students each at 6 different stops. How many students are now on the bus?

As you can see, the answer lends itself to multiple approaches, allowing internal differentiation. Some students will create addition problems, others subtraction, others multiplication, and so on. This allows a teacher to see students' comfort level with the concepts and can be used to assess next steps for each student. The teacher can also challenge students who are ready for more to create additional problems, perhaps with specific guidance:

- Can you make a problem involving division?
- Can you make one with fractions?
- Make a game with your answers, using a pattern.
- Make your problems into a real story with a beginning, middle, and ending.
- Show how someone might solve your problem using drawings.
- Show a solution using manipulatives.

So while students who may be struggling with language or basic operations can take their time to develop their skills, the students who are ready for more are challenged at their own levels and not being turned off by math through boredom. The possibilities are endless!

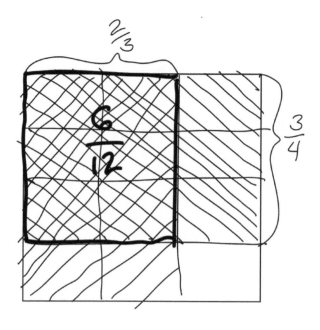

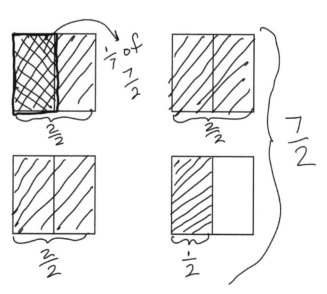

Figure 5.5. Two different student work products showing fraction multiplication.

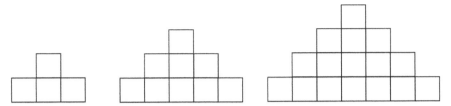

Figure 5.6. Pattern of squares for algebraic thinking.

DISCUSSION STRATEGIES FOR PROBLEM SOLVING

Note to the reader: This section is most relevant for teachers who have class-rooms of students, rather than homeschooling parents. If you don't have a classroom, it might be interesting to think about your own schooling and how you think about what education should look like while you read, however.

In the early 2010s, a fellow trainer shared this exercise, which you, reader, are encouraged to try:

Challenge the participants in the workshop to remember all the names of the seven dwarfs in Snow White without using any external resources, like the internet.

Set a timer for one minute and write as many of Disney's seven dwarfs' names as you can.

1. _____
2. _____
3. _____
4. _____
5. _____
6. _____
7. _____

Like most workshop participants, you probably remembered between one and five dwarf names.

Now, still without any search engines or internet access, find a learning partner or two. They can be family member in the same house, fellow teachers in the break room, or someone you call by phone. Give them the same challenge: in one minute, name as many of the seven dwarfs as you can.

After one minute, share your answers. In the workshops, participants would get two minutes to discuss the question with a partner or a group. After the discussion, did you get all seven? If not, did you get at least more than you did alone?

In the workshops, more people would have collected all seven names. In all cases, they would have a higher number afterward (unless someone already remembered all seven, which never happened in these workshops).

This is a powerful demonstration of how collaboration helps people to learn more, or at least access more knowledge. Chances are that after this activity, the participants would remember more names the next time they were asked. Even the most traditional teachers are often impressed by the power of this, because it shows the power of discussion about knowledge.

In the past, math classes were expected to be either silent (with students working independently) or with only one voice heard, either that of the teacher or of the student the teacher had called upon. However, the most effective math teaching happens when students can speak their thoughts aloud.

What if, instead of, "Math classes should be silent," we changed it to, "Math classes should *almost never* be silent"? In other words, what if the vast majority of math classes were discussion based?

How do we change from the traditional paradigm to encouraging discussion without chaos erupting? That's the biggest fear most teachers face when changing their modalities.

Fortunately, there are multiple proven ways to make these changes with protocols and routines. Protocols and routines provide frameworks in which discussion can happen in a structured way, meaning both teachers and students have expectations about how class will proceed. There are many high-quality books and training resources outside of this one that go into the routines in more depth. This book will describe some of the routines to give the reader an idea of what they are like; these are routines the author has personally experienced and trained teachers to implement.

Before looking at the routines, there are a few important notions to keep in mind:

1. Different students think and process at different speeds. Faster doesn't mean smarter or better. The protocols should allow for *wait time*, or time for students to process their ideas. For students who process quickly, they can be challenged to deepen or extend their thinking by challenges such as finding additional strategies or explaining or applying their thinking.

2. Math classes have had a tendency to group students into similar ability groupings, or leveling, in the name of differentiation. However, as was explored in the "Middle Childhood" chapter, this reinforces an ability mindset. In addition, if you ask students to tackle problems with other students of the same ability, not much learning will happen. Imagine grouping the teachers asked about the seven dwarfs into groups that

knew one or none, and groups that knew all seven. The first group could get stuck quickly (unless they all knew different ones), and the other group would be bored because they solved the question too quickly.

Instead, consider grouping students heterogeneously (with apparently different ability levels) when they are expected to work together. Homogeneous (apparently same ability levels) grouping has its place, but not usually in these discussion protocols.

The protocols reviewed here include number talks, five practices, reciprocal teaching, and Socratic seminar.

Number Talks

This is a protocol that can be used with any mental math problem, situation, or pattern.

An example of how it might sound at the beginning is given in the earlier dialogue between the teacher, Joseph, and Aleah. The teacher presents the mental math problem, pattern, or situation. The students have time to think with a closed fist over their heart. As they think of one way to solve it, they extend their thumb away from their fist, still on their chest. As they think of additional ways, they extend more fingers. This allows the teacher to monitor student thinking and readiness, and it engages all students.

Why is this better than raising hands? When students raise hands, it often comes with a pressure to answer, and they often feel discouraged if they want to answer and aren't chosen. Others can feel like they want to hide and don't want to participate, and if they are called upon when their hands are down, they can feel resentful.

When the students use a fist with fingers showing the number of solution strategies, first, the fist isn't usually visible to too many others besides the teacher. This lends an element of privacy and can make slower-processing students feel less embarrassed.

Second, it also allows the teacher to measure and institute the right amount of wait time, and students with fewer answers can be engaged first so they have a chance to speak.

Third, teachers can use the students with more answers to differentiate and extend the students' thinking with new or more sophisticated strategies. There is more on this later.

Imagine another example: 6 + 8. This sounds simple, right? Now think of as many ways as you can to solve this. If a learning partner is available, include them in the conversation about the different ways to solve it. Then share how many ways you had in common, and how many were new for each of you.

Some examples of solution strategies might be:

- I made a 10 by moving two from the six and making it 4 + 10. That makes 14.
- I found the fives in the two numbers and broke out the rest, so it was 5 + 1 + 5 + 3, or 5 + 5 + 1 + 3, or 10 + 4, so 14.
- I took beans and arranged them into groups of 5 plus what was left over, so 14.
- I know my doubles, so I moved one from the 8 and made it 7 + 7, so 14.

If none of the students has provided your strategy, the teacher can partici-pate as well. It's important that this is done in a participatory way and not with the implication of "This is the right way to do it." If after sharing your way, you find that a number of students start doing it your way, chances are they are following an authority model. In that case, it's best for the teacher to refrain from sharing for a while until students gain confidence in their own strategies.

As mentioned earlier, when all students have at least a thumb extended, the teacher can encourage participation from those who normally would be missed because of their processing speed by calling on the thumb-only stu-dents first. Then after those are finished, the students whose ways haven't been named, who may have multiple strategies, can share. This will lead to more listening and learning by all.

Why is this? The students who are slower to process often don't get a voice in traditional math classes. This protocol gives them space to share and can help to build their confidence. It also forces the speedier ones to slow down and listen to see if their strategy was already shared. Then it gives space for those with perhaps greater speed and versatility to share their unique thinking after the heightened emotions of initial sharing are over, leaving those who may have less confidence some space to listen and learn.

A good question to end a number talk is, "What are some ways to solve this that *none* of us has thought of?"

Five Practices for Orchestrating Productive Mathematics Discussions

This protocol has developed over years, and there is now more than one edition of the flagship book about the practice. The five practices are, after determining the objective and selecting the task, anticipating, monitoring, selecting, sequencing, and connecting.

The process involves, first of all, identification of a learning objective that the teacher knows how to measure. Then follows careful preparation of a single task for the students to investigate.

Part of the teacher's preparation is anticipating the students' strategies and misconceptions that would appear with this task. As the students work, the teacher monitors the students for the expected strategies and misconceptions, as well as new ones, often recording their thoughts on a monitoring sheet where they have recorded their anticipations. As the task proceeds, the teacher selects approaches to share and develops a sequence of sharing to maximize learning. Finally, they facilitate a discussion wherein students make connections between concepts and between the strategies they shared.

This set of practices is highly skilled, as it requires teachers to make wise decisions on the spot in the classroom based on student responses. The teacher's work is not the traditional lecture-and-call-upon; instead, the teacher facilitates and monitors the student discussions, considering carefully who should present their ideas after the discussion is over to maximize the students learning from each other. It requires practice, and training beforehand is ideal; at the very least, reading the book is a must.

Reciprocal Teaching

This is a set of practices based on reciprocal reading, in which students are responsible for working productively in groups. The roles for reciprocal reading are not quite the same as those for reciprocal math; there are some collaboratively developed role definitions that seem to work well for students, especially those in late elementary school (grade four) and older. A copy of the guidance cards created collaboratively with multiple teachers in several schools can be found in the Resources section of the author's website. These include questions to guide students in understanding their roles.

If a teacher is using reciprocal reading in the classroom, this is a good protocol for students to transfer their skills to math. These roles work well when students are given a specific challenging task or problem to complete. Each role has specific guidelines, and students can take on one or more roles, depending on group size. The facilitator encourages the students to act out their roles, which helps prevent the tendency for one or two students to carry a group.

The roles can be distributed among up to eight students, or each student can carry more than one role. Groups of more than five tend to be unwieldy, so with groups of four, students can each take two roles. The students work on the problem together to understand and solve it. The roles should rotate among students in different groupings so everyone has the opportunity to play each role.

The roles are:

- Clarifying: Ensuring that all group members understand all parts of the question
- Predicting: Depending on the problem, this might mean facilitating the group in anticipating strategies, estimating what the answer might be and/or what would be reasonable or not for an answer
- Connecting: Helping all group members connect to prior knowledge and/or real-world context
- Visualizing: Supporting the group in picturing what the problem or situation is about, including drawings if called for
- Questioning: Facilitating group questions by asking them and encouraging them in others
- Solving: Supporting solution strategies within the group; ensuring that all parts are answered
- Summarizing: Reviewing the work done, the different strategies, and the ways the answers connect to the question
- Reflecting: Asking if the answers are reasonable, how they were the same or different from the predictions, and what the group learned from this work

This may seem like a lot for a group to take on. Instead of doing all roles at once, the roles can be introduced one at a time or a few at a time and practiced until the students are comfortable with them. Later, more roles can be introduced. Again, this may be most useful in schools where reciprocal reading is already being used.

Socratic Seminar

This is the most advanced of the approaches in this section. There are many possible structures under this umbrella as well. While the structures may differ, what remains the same is that the students learn to lead the discussions themselves, without teacher guidance or feedback; the teacher's role is to facilitate a deepening process by questioning and keep it from going off the rails.

Let's return to one of the pitfalls we already discussed. Students traditionally look to the teacher for everything: the answer, hints, guidance, discipline, and all kinds of structure. Students will even look to teachers for cues about whether or not something is funny.

Part of the key to a successful Socratic seminar is weaning students off this tendency. One way to do this is for the teacher to develop a poker face during the seminar. This can be challenging for teachers; one way to make this happen is to task oneself to record different interactions in the seminar. For example, tally marks can be used to track different types of participation: statements, procedures, questions, or reading text. Engaging in this non-inferential feedback can keep a teacher busy with their head down and not available for students to take their cues from the teacher's expression.

One example of how a Socratic seminar in math might look is that the teacher provides a pattern for students to examine. Many such patterns are available on Youcubed[4] and nrich.maths.org. The students may have the opportunity to study and attempt the task at home or prior to the seminar; classes that are more experienced with this model may attempt it without prior study.

If the teachers don't have access to training, the recommended resource to start implementing this protocol is *The Power of the Socratic Classroom* by Charles Fischer.

In summary, all the protocols described here are scaffolds, or supports, for developing productive group work in the classroom. A teacher may decide to use one or several of them. The goal is eventually that students will develop the ability to work productively in groups without a scaffold or protocol, encouraging all voices and working together to achieve more than they could have on their own.

LANGUAGE ROUTINES FOR PROBLEM SOLVING

One of the biggest challenges in learning math is language, which has an important place in mathematical development from an early age, as earlier chapters have illustrated. Not only do students often come with language challenges due to delayed reading or learning disabilities, but also, many classrooms have at least a few English language learners. To help students overcome these challenges, Stanford University developed a set of language routines, called mathematical language routines (MLRs).[5]

While the original document is designed for principles of curriculum design for English language learners, the activities they lead to are engaging and deepening, and they are excellent for any classroom. This section will illustrate what two of them might look like in practice.

MLR 5: Co-craft Questions and Problems

As we saw in chapter 4, the main reason for introducing word problems is to provide context for mathematics that would appear in life, and to make the math more relevant to students.

For classrooms that are textbook and workbook bound, word problems remain a chore that students need to get through. Besides creative ways of making the completion of the work more fun, which are possible using strategies like those found in Katie Powell's *Boredom Busters*, the teacher's primary charge is to make the situations meaningful. This is how connections to real-life situations can develop.

This MLR says, in part:

> *Through this routine, students are able to use conversation skills to generate, choose (argue for the best one), and improve questions, problems, and situations as well as develop meta-awareness of the language used in mathematical questions and problems. Teachers should push for clarity and revoice oral responses as necessary.*[6]

Imagine you are teaching seventh-grade students about solving equations using positive and negative integers.[7] The word problem on the page reads as follows:

The temperature on Tuesday reached a high of 85 degrees F. At night, it fell 28 degrees. The next morning, it only went up 17 degrees. What was the temperature on Wednesday?

To co-craft questions, present the situation without the question at the end. The students would see:

The temperature on Tuesday reached a high of 85 degrees F. At night, it fell 28 degrees. The next morning, it only went up 17 degrees.

At this point, ask the students, "What questions can you come up with about this situation?" The students have a few minutes to create their own questions. Then they can turn and talk to a partner, or a group, and come up with a favorite question. The whole class will then share their questions, which can be recorded on a piece of paper or whiteboard. Examples of student questions could include:

- What was the difference between Tuesday's temperature and Wednesday's?
- What was Wednesday's temperature?
- What was the difference between how much it fell and how much it went up?
- What season is it?

Then the class can discuss which question merits solving. The last one, "What season is it?," might be fun to guess but doesn't really relate to the objective. The second, "What was Wednesday's temperature?," is worded differently than the original question, but it asks the same question. Using the students' wording instead of the textbook's or teacher's is validating and connecting for the students and makes no difference in reaching the objective.

Another advantage of this approach is that the students themselves create opportunity for differentiation, or ways to engage those who are struggling and those who are more advanced in the concept. The first and third questions can be kept for this differentiation.

The first question, "What was the difference between Tuesday's temperature and Wednesday's?," is a multistep problem that requires solving for Wednesday's temperature before answering it. The third question is a simple subtraction problem, $28 - 17$. For struggling learners, the third question might be a first step into the problem before they think about solving for Wednesday's temperature.

Co-crafting problems is similar, but it involves generalizing knowledge on the students' part. In this, students are asked to create new situations that are similar to other problems. With the temperature example above, students might work alone or in pairs to create similar problems. These might be temperature change situations with different numbers, or there might be similar numbers with different situations, or the problems might be completely different altogether. The guideline would be that the questions would need to reach the educational objective of equations with integers.

Some examples of co-crafted problems by students could be:

- The temperature on Friday got down to 20 degrees. The next day, it went up 14 degrees, and then on Sunday, it went down another 32 degrees. What was the temperature on Sunday?
- Mikayla had $90. She spent $35 on food for her and her friend. After that, her parents gave her $23 allowance. How much money did she end up with?
- A game had the following rolls of different dice: 16, 19, 2, 14, 12. If you have to start out with positive numbers and switch to negative on the next number, so 16, -19, 2, -14, 12, what's the final sum?

After students create and solve their own problems, they can trade with a partner and solve each other's problems. This provides an opportunity for additional practice on the concept in an interesting way as well as a way for each student to check that they made and solved their own question correctly. Creating these problems also supports critical thinking in multiple-choice tests, because by writing their own questions, students are more likely to identify distractors and incorrect answers on standardized tests.

A classroom that does this regularly can assemble the problems the class agrees are best, and they can publish the book for their own classroom use, or even for the wider world. Alternatively, students can collect their own authored problems and use them either as a portfolio collection or a book-let they self-publish. Either way, this is an excellent integration with good principles of literacy and will create more ownership and understanding in the students.

MLR 6: Three Reads

Many student errors come from not reading or fully comprehending text, especially with complex word problems. Therefore, the tendency by many teachers and curricula has been to remove language and mathematical com-plexity to improve performance. However, this reduces the level of rigor in the math and, because of this, the skill level possibility of the students. The greater the opportunity to tackle challenging work, the more the children grow; higher expectations lead to higher performance.

One example of this MLR is written as follows in the Stanford document:

Students are supported in reading a situation/problem three times, each time with a particular focus:

1. *Students read the situation with the goal of comprehending the text (describe the situation without using numbers).*
2. *Students read the situation with the goal of analyzing the language used to present the mathematical structure.*
3. *Students read the situation in order to brainstorm possible mathemati-cal solution methods.*[8]

For the first read, the essential part of it is reading the question without numbers. For example, consider the following problem.

Using three reads, read the problem the first time like this:

Marcus has some pens. Elaine has fewer pens than Marcus. Pedro has more pens than Elaine.

Do you notice how the problem gets easier to visualize when read this way? As we saw earlier in this chapter, visualization is key to problem solv-ing, and students with special needs have greater challenges visualizing than regular-education students. Teachers can support student learning by asking questions about the story situation to support visualization, for example, "Can you see the pens? What kinds of pens? What does Marcus look like? How old is Elaine? Can you imagine that they all have different pens, and how they look together?"

Once the students can picture the situation in their minds, they can draw the situation using bar models or other models if they choose to help them solve the problem. In this next step, the problem is read as originally written, but pauses can be added for processing. For example, after "Elaine has 3 fewer pens than Marcus," the teacher or students can ask, "Can you see what that looks like? Who has more pens?"

In the next sentence, "Pedro has twice as many pens as Elaine," a drawing that shows that literally can be helpful. The students can draw Elaine's pens twice. Stacking the bars in comparison problems can be helpful, as we saw with Pete's and Marnie's pennies; analyzing the language, with the words *fewer* and *twice as many* indicating comparison, will give the cues to direct student thinking. The question indicates a collection of all together, so a bracket grouping all three models can be helpful.

Now that students have understood the problem and visualized it with the numbers, they can brainstorm solution strategies. Some might choose to add all the numbers together; others might use subtraction and multiplication as part of their strategy. Still others might need to use counters. Whatever the approach, the students can and should find their own ways. Sharing strategies after the solutions will lead to learning by all, including the teacher, who will gain insight into each student's thinking and how they can be challenged productively.

For teachers, reading this may fly in the face of their training to use other strategies such as CUBES, where students are encouraged to "Circle numbers, Underline the question, Box the keywords, Eliminate extra information, and

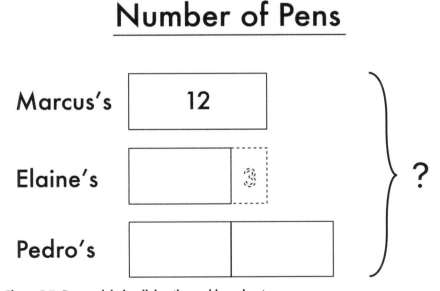

Number of Pens

Marcus's — 12

Elaine's

Pedro's

?

Figure 5.7. Bar model visualizing the problem about pens.

Solve." In contrast to the visualization approaches, this procedure encourages hyperfocus on details and dissection of the problem into parts.

Unfortunately, this can lead to common mistakes, such as students defaulting to known operations on the numbers or being misled by "keywords" to the wrong strategies. Many tests are designed to capitalize on these weaknesses, which leads to lower test scores.

Why do teachers implement mnemonics like CUBES? Does research support it? Unfortunately, like many such approaches, it has spread widely through the teaching world without solid research upholding it. Looking for solutions is understandable, because without teachers knowing research-based approaches, word problems can seem opaque and unreachable. But while CUBES may improve outcomes better than no strategy at all, it doesn't compare well to many of the strategies developed and supported by research.

The other major issue here is the reliance on "keywords." While having a strong mathematical vocabulary (Standard of Mathematical Practice 6: "Attend to precision") is essential, keywords tend to have the opposite effect. Rather than lending meaning to the mathematical processes, keywords become like a magic spell that the user can incant to unlock the problem.[9] The trouble is, the results are often undesired.

Take, for example, teaching that "in all" means "add." Then read this problem:

Renee has 15 pens. John has 7 pens. How many pens do they have in all?

It works for that one, right?
But then try this one:

Renee has 28 pens. John has 3 times as many pens as Renee. How many pens do they have in all?

What mistake can you anticipate based on the keyword strategy? You may realize that the majority of keyword-based students will answer "31 pens." Why? Because "in all" means "add," and the only numbers present in the problem are 28 and 3. If they're using CUBES, they circled the numbers and boxed the keywords; that will lead them find the sum of the two numbers in the problem, without realizing the 3 represents a multiplier and not an addend.

What a mess. Not only is this problem a two-step problem, it also requires multiplication *before* addition! This is only one example of how students can be led astray by such approaches.

In the bigger picture, Standard of Mathematical Practice 1 says, "Make sense of problems and persevere in solving them."[10] If word problems are seen as a situation requiring a particular formula, such as CUBES, in the habitual approach to solving them, there is no sense-making; there is only application of the formula. It also means students are less likely to be able to generalize their solutions to real-world problems. Since the whole reason for word problems is to create relevant problem-solving situations, using hyperfocus strategies defeats that purpose.

For homeschooling parents, classes with hybrid or remote instruction, or classes that utilize technology for homework, Desmos[11] has a number of wonderful math lessons and activities that utilize interaction and feedback by text. Teachers can also design their own lessons using their digital tools. This medium is excellent for those who communicate better by the written word, and it helps those who are learning to express themselves in writing as well.

Important Practices

- Provide lots of opportunities for productive struggle in problem solving.
- Give students tools to visualize the math.
- Practice model drawing that leads to schematic visualization.
- Provide open-ended problem-solving opportunities.
- Give students many opportunities to discuss the math with each other.
- Have students co-craft questions and problems.
- Read the problems multiple times and in different ways, including without the numbers.
- Avoid problem-solving approaches that promote hyperfocus and/or dissection of the problem over making sense of the problem.
- Utilize technology appropriately to facilitate written discussion.

What is a problem in your own life that you could reapproach with some of these strategies?

The author uses some of these strategies when considering a household budget.

NOTES

1. Thinking blocks apps are available at https://www.mathplayground.com/thinkingblocks.html.

2. While EngageNY no longer hosts Eureka Math, the original version is still available for free at unbounded.org. The free and paid versions can both be found at greatminds.org after signing up for an account.

3. Patterns are available on youcubed.org for free.

4. Youcubed.org also has many tasks that are free to use.

5. Jeff Zwiers et al., *Principles for the Design of Mathematics Curricula: Promoting Language* and *Content Development*, Understanding Language/Stanford Center for Assessment, Learning and Equity at Stanford University. 2017. https://ul.stanford.edu/sites/default/files/resource/2021-11/Principles%20for%20the%20Design%20of%20Mathematics%20Curricula_1.pdf.

6. Zwiers et al., *Principles for the Design*, 14.

7. Mathematical Content Standard 7.EE.3.B: "Solve multistep real-life and mathematical problems posed with positive and negative rational numbers in any form (whole numbers, fractions, and decimals), using tools strategically. Apply properties of operations to calculate with numbers in any form; convert between forms as appropriate; and assess the reasonableness of answers using mental computation and estimation strategies."

8. Zwiers et al., *Principles for the Design*, 15.

9. See Margie Pearse's blog article on the topic: "Word Problems Are More Than Magic," *Corwin Connect* (blog), May 11, 2016, https://corwin-connect.com/2016/05/word-problems-magic/.

10. Common Core Standards Writing Team, *Progressions for the Common Core State Standards for Mathematics* (Tucson: Institute for Mathematics and Education, University of Arizona, 2022), https://mathematicalmusings.org/wp-content/uploads/2023/02/Progressions.pdf, 303.

11. Sign up at teacher.desmos.com.

Chapter 6

Middle School

Synthesis and Gaps

I've never run into a person who yearns for their middle school days.—
Jeff Kinney

Middle school! The very words conjure memories of traumatizing experiences in so many people. Hazing, bullying, adolescent awkwardness, popularity, cliques, hormones, menstruation, fighting, identity seeking—and so much more—are all entering the picture for previously innocent children. Add this to the increased independence, responsibility, and homework loads they experience, and students can struggle like they have never struggled before.

While the children faced irrationality in previous stages of childhood, now they are encountering whole new levels of chaos in themselves. Their bodies are changing, their brains are developing, and peers take the place of authority in their social structures rather than the adults in their lives.

Teachers themselves have to be a special breed to want to work at this level. When Yahoo groups were popular, a large one was titled, "I'm Crazy, I Teach Middle School." This group provided support to the brave souls who encounter the unpredictable, creative, exciting mess these ages involve. The name of the group captured the mentality a teacher needs to have to enjoy teaching middle school. This is also often the age homeschooling parents give up homeschooling, because it gets more difficult to educate your own willful tweens and teens.

In chapter 3, we learned about how texts can overscaffold problem solving, and that teachers can end up doing this as well. Since middle school is usually the time when students solidify their identities about being "good or bad" at math, it's especially important here to consider *differentiation* and how to approach it.

One approach to differentiation is to provide different materials to different students. The idea behind this is to provide access to the students at the level they can succeed; it uses the idea of the zone of proximal development, as explained earlier.

Let's explore the idea of ZPD in a different way from the previous chapter.

Consider moving to a new country as an adult where you speak none of the language. Staying in your comfort level means you seek out people and places where your native tongue is exclusively spoken and written. The frustration level is trying to enter society without any background or foundational language learning with people who don't know your language. Staying in the ZPD could mean entering the society with translators, apps, language classes, and other supports to help you bridge your way into the new language.

This can be illustrated by the story of "egg and da chips."

In the seventies, a man immigrated to London without knowing any English. He needed food, so he asked his cousin to teach him something to order. The cousin told him, "Order egg and chips."

So the man went to the corner shop and ordered "egg and da chips." To his delight, he received a fried egg and chips, or fries.

He continued ordering "egg and da chips" every morning for a week, but then he became tired of the same order, so he asked his cousin to teach him the words for different food. His cousin taught him "egg and toast."

This time, when he went to order "egg and da toast," the cashier asked him, "White or wheat?"

The man was stumped. What did that mean? After an awkward pause, he blurted, "Egg and da chips!"

This man reverted to his comfort zone, like so many do when they are challenged to frustration. Had he had some kind of support, like someone to translate, a translation device, or even pictures of what the different orders could be, he could have grown his repertoire and, at the very least, improved his level of nourishment.

One of the major problems with giving students different materials according to their learning levels is that it keeps students where they are, or *tracks* them. Tracking, introduced by the Prussian system of education, is when students are placed in classes according to their perceived learning levels. Unlike with language classes, where the level follows a set sequence as well as assessments, tracked math classes can begin early in school, identifying advanced, grade-level, or remedial students.

Tracking is popular in many European-influenced school systems, among others. It's like a class system that gets applied to learning ability, with little mobility possible between the different levels. In middle and high school, if the school uses tracking, a student on the low, middle, or high ramp has little opportunity to change. The "low" students are given a lower ramp, so they never reach the higher levels. The "high" students go on a different journey, and if they start to struggle, they face the mindset issues of feeling like a failure because they aren't able to sustain the performance. Often this leads to hiring outside tutors or doing other outside work to sustain the track.

Salman Khan, the founder of Khan Academy, addresses some of the issues with tracking in his 2012 book *The One World Schoolhouse*.[1] He describes how in a summer program that implemented his developing software, some of the students who started out lowest rose to the top of the class by the end of the program. He attributes this to the fact that his program is adaptive, meaning it identifies strengths, gaps, and weaknesses in learning, and gives students targeted lessons and practice to close gaps and strengthen weaknesses while spending less time on their strengths. Later implementation in schools has borne out the success of providing opportunities to close gaps in an adaptive program.

In the summer program, one girl he called Marcela started out very low and worked slowly through the content in the first half of the summer. In the second half, something clicked, and she accelerated to be the second most advanced in the program. She was able to grasp complex concepts that her peers could not, as well. Had she remained in a tracked program, her mathematical intuition would not have had a chance to flower; this software allowed her to close gaps from her previous schooling and not only catch up to, but exceed, grade-level expectations. This can make or break a person's perception of themselves and their possibility in life.

Since that time, many other adaptive programs have been developed, but Khan Academy remains a high-quality, free program for anyone, including adults, to use to progress their learning. It has also had a pivotal influence in the use of data to inform instruction, meaning using what the students know and don't know to provide more effective teaching.

In the classroom, while some students, including those with major gaps or learning issues, will need very scaffolded materials, a different and often more effective approach is using "low-floor, high-ceiling tasks." What this means is that the task is available to all learners, whether students are at a rudimentary level in that area or are capable of more complex thinking about the topic.

When such tasks are provided to heterogeneous, or mixed-ability, groupings, a great deal of learning can happen. Not only do the complex thinkers provide clever ways for the others to consider, but the simpler ways often illustrate creative or visual ways of thinking that the abstract thinkers couldn't access on their own. This provides enrichment and meaning all around.

A key part of an environment that fosters this kind of collaboration is growth mindset, as discussed in the "Middle Childhood" chapter. This means, importantly, that there is no competition in the learning.

When students are developing an identity in middle school, competition can be a big part of this development. Middle school students can be cutthroat in their desire to be on the top of the school social hierarchy. Depending on the school culture, that can lead to either more competition in academics or peer pressure to not be too academic.

Therefore, math class could provide an opportunity for a safe space in which everyone can excel and be supported to grow at their own pace. Given the chaos and pressures upon students described at the beginning of the chapter, this can be crucial to a student's future in math, or even in school.

How might this look? Let's illustrate this with a true story.

In a middle school in the Bronx with a minority and low-income population, the school had integrated classes with regular- and special-ed students and one self-contained class for each grade. The integrated classes had two teachers, a regular-ed and a special-ed teacher. The self-contained classrooms, with one special-ed teacher, were for a small number of students whose special needs were deemed too great for integration into a regular-ed classroom. While this is not the same as the heterogeneous setting recommended earlier, the high needs of the setting help to illustrate how important a classroom culture can be.

As you can imagine, the students in the self-contained class had a low self-image. This would lead to disruptions in learning that would include acting out, refusal to participate, cutting class, and more.

A sixth-grade teacher who began to implement some of the approaches in this book early in the year saw tremendous success in turning the behaviors around. Many of the students came in with second- or third-grade-level math skills. By using manipulatives to introduce grade-level content, and following the concrete-pictorial-abstract progression described earlier, students with rudimentary understanding were able to develop their understanding and skills to close gaps quickly.

Take, for example, introducing positive and negative numbers, a sixth-grade standard. In most schools, that would begin with a number line. However, a number line is a pictorial representation that's too abstract for some minds to grasp as a first introduction.

Instead, the teacher used double-sided counters, with the red side representing negative one and yellow representing one, to encourage students to explore how numbers can be built. Combining the counters so that a one and a negative one make zero, otherwise known as a *zero pair*, provided a foundation for understanding how it works.

This can also lead to another revelation: all positive numbers are sums of ones, and all negative numbers are sums of negative ones. Students who were taught numbers in isolation, without this foundational understanding, can develop more flexibility with this approach.

Then a number line made of tape with sticky notes representing numbers was laid on the floor, with a corresponding Walking the Number Line activity from GeoGebra[2] on the interactive whiteboard. The line of tape stretched from one long end of the room to the other. A small piece of tape was added perpendicularly to mark zero, with a corresponding sticky notes showing the number. More marks were added to either side, following the lines between the tiles to support equal spacing. The sticky notes with their corresponding numbers from one to ten and negative one to negative ten were added as well.

When a mathematical expression from the simulation was shown on the interactive whiteboard, a student would use their body to act out the situation with other students calling out guidance, meaning they would turn and walk their body along the number line appropriately to the expression. The seated students would simultaneously model the situation using the counters. With these three representations at once, the students were able to access and grasp the concept using what they knew.

This was a low-floor, high-ceiling approach to the task because students who were still grasping how numbers work could use counters, others could use the visualization of the number line, and still others could compute abstractly.

The teacher also fostered a safe place by doing number talks, introduced in chapter 5, regularly. She would encourage students to share their thinking about a basic math situation, pattern, or picture and record the student responses on easel paper. This led to calm validation of student thinking and allowed the fears of being seen to be inadequate to stay outside the classroom.

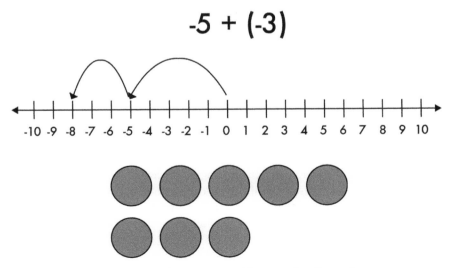

Figure 6.1. An integer expression represented by a number line and counters.

Some students would approach the tasks simply while others used more advanced approaches; all benefited from learning from each other.

When a visitor would walk into the small classroom, instead of the hostility and fear that would meet them at the start of the year, the visitor would be welcomed. The students listened to and encouraged each other—a rarity in this community. The room was calm, peaceful, joyful, and a safe space. Real learning was happening there.

As the school year went on and the students grew, the principal exclaimed that if she had been taught math the way this teacher was teaching it, she would have understood and enjoyed it so much more.

USING PATTERNS TO LEARN

Have you ever tried to boil math down to its core two understandings? In discussions with teachers, this question leads to a lot of fascinating discourse. If you wish, try to answer the question here without using the internet. For those using this chapter in professional learning, this is an opportunity to try this exercise together.

What are the two core elements of mathematics (one word each)?

_____   _____

When adults are asked what math is about, they often come up with answers like computation, analysis, problem solving, or numbers. While these are all true, they lie on the middle to outer parts of mathematics. If these resemble your answers and you'd like to challenge yourself, try asking more questions.

- Why do we compute?
- Where does computation come from?
- What are we analyzing?
- What is the core of problem solving?
- What do numbers, counting, and so forth represent?

Did you identify that one of the core elements of mathematics is *patterns*? Let's explore!

If you look carefully at what's happening in mathematics, starting as basic as what numbers are, patterns will begin to jump out at you. The pattern of counting numbers follows the sequence of adding one more. In our base-ten system, we restart the pattern of zero through nine every decade of counting (tens, twenties, thirties, etc.).

Fractions follow patterns as well. Unlike the whole numbers, where the next numeral in sequence represents a higher value, denominators represent smaller unit sizes as the numeral increases. So unlike two, three, four, five, six, and so on, where the next one in the series represents an increase, ½, ⅓, ¼, ⅕, ⅙, and so on represent decreases, respectively.

This can be confusing even to middle schoolers. Fraction computation is a major focus in grades five and six, so teachers should not be shy about breaking out the fraction tiles to support understanding. Chapter 7 explores this in greater depth.

One characteristic of middle school students is that they are easily bored. Teachers are warring with the competing interests of hormone-induced fascinations and other social concerns. Therefore, introducing mathematics in novel ways and with relevant connections to real life will be more likely to engage the students in mathematics.

For example, students can learn about different bases by introducing a binary concept through the fact that this is how their phones and computers think. All these machines have is one or zero, and all of ones and zeros combine in many clever ways to make the powerful device they can carry in their hands. Students can imagine, therefore, how much computing power is in a being, a human, who can think not only in zero through nine, but through all the letters of the alphabet and imagery as well!

This can be a fantastic and fun introduction to computer science and powers of two. For example, ask students to look at the following sequence: 1, 2, 4, 8, 16, 32, 64, 128, 256, 512, 1024, and so on.

Then ask if they recognize any of those numbers from daily life. Some might call out that those are options in RAM, or memory, for phones, laptops, and so on, in gigabytes or even terabytes.

Therefore, a laptop with a half-gig drive doesn't actually have 500 GB, even though the marketing materials might call it that; instead, it's 512.

Next, ask students if they notice a pattern in the numbers in relation to each other. This can be done in partners or small groups, then as a whole-group share. Some students will say all the numbers except 1 are even. Others might say that each one doubles the previous number. Still others could talk about how quickly the numbers grow. Then there might be some who talk about multiplication or exponents.

This is another example of a low-floor, high-ceiling access to a concept. Different students will use their grasp of numbers in different ways as their own way in. As the discussion proceeds, students will construct their understanding of what base two involves and how it works.

Another productive challenge is around base twelve. Ask students to think of ways we might count in twelves. They might mention twelve hours in a day, twelve months in a year, twelve eggs in a dozen, or twelve inches in a foot.

While our counting system is based on tens because that's the number of digits we have, there's another counting system that uses the fingers almost like an abacus. Shepherds used it to track sheep, and it can be found all over the world. It works like this:

Counting begins by using the thumb of one hand to touching each phalanx (finger section) on the fingers of the same hand. The thumb touches the top, middle, and bottom phalanges, making three; with four fingers, this leads to a maximum of twelve phalanges. The numbers of twelves are tracked in a similar way using the phalanges on the other hand. The first phalanx stands for 12, the next two twelves, or 24, the third, 36; with four phalanges, there is a maximum of twelve times twelve, or 144, otherwise known as a gross.

Try giving students a large number of objects to count and encouraging them to count the items this way. It's fun and engaging, and it might come in handy in the future. In addition, identifying, analyzing, and discussing the differences between base ten and base twelve can help students avoid common errors in measurement systems such as imperial length and counting time units.

Let's look at another way patterns can be helpful. Traditional American pre-algebra and algebra programs introduce linear equations with the slope-intercept form of an equation and how to interpret that from a graph, as well as how to graph the line and make a table of values. There is little to no discussion about why this is important to learn, where these concepts came from, or even the connections to other forms of the equation, and why slope-intercept form is helpful. The discussions or materials may exist in the text, but without the foundation for understanding it, many teachers and homeschooling parents skip right over those. So let's get into it.

First, let's talk about the question at the start of this section. We've discussed how *patterns* are one core element of mathematics. What's the second one? Have you figured it out yet? Yes, it's *connections*! Connections are such an important part of learning math, as we've seen from earlier chapters that illustrate both the historical roots of mathematics and the way connections are formed as we learn. We will need both patterns and connections as we go through the following exercises that are designed to illustrate these principles. Feel free to follow along and try them as you read.

For beginning equation-makers, start by drawing a pattern of circles. Draw one circle with a number 1 underneath, two circles with a number 2 underneath, three with a 3, and so on, up to about five. Students should notice that the number corresponds with the count of circles, like in Figure 6.2.

Ask them what the pattern is. Then ask them to write an equation that works for every value in the series. They should come up with number of count = total circles, $n = c$, or some such variation.

Next, increase the challenge. What happens if you start with two circles and add one each time?

This is the same sequence, but with c (circles) = n (counting number) + 1 (or whatever variables they choose). Ask them to test their equation by finding the number of circles at count 10.

Continue the pattern with two, four, six, eight circles ($c = 2n$) and then three, five, seven, nine circles ($c = 2n + 1$). Each time, ask them to find the number of circles at the tenth count, and then check if they're right by drawing the pattern.

By now, students should start to be able to see that finding the pattern and writing an equation for it allows them to predict the value without having to draw every single circle.

Let's apply this to real-life scenarios. Ask the students to imagine they started saving $7 every month, and they never spent any of that money. Ask them to find out the total in one year. That's easy to predict. But then ask them to find how many months it will take for them to afford a game system they're saving toward if it costs $300. Again, this can be simple division, but it's a bit more challenging.

Finally, ask them to find how much faster they'd afford the game system if they saved $9 every month rather than $7. This is a two-step problem, both using the division and then subtracting one quotient from another, and applying it to real life (not partial months).

This is a good point to introduce graphing. Using technology tools such as GeoGebra or Desmos, ask them to graph the first situation. Discuss with them what they notice about the graph. They should notice that the line goes up steeply and crosses through the origin. Ask them if the negative values have any meaning here, and if they apply to the situation. This can be a good opportunity to introduce *domain* and *range*;[3] if the domain only includes positive numbers, the graph is restricted to the gains.

Then ask them to find where the line crosses 300 on the y-axis. They should see that it's around 43 on the x-axis.

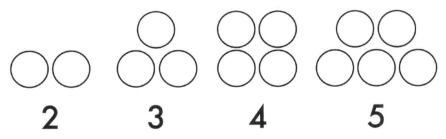

2   3   4   5

Figure 6.2.   The first pattern of circles.

Now let's make a connection to why we see equations so often in terms of x and y. Students should observe that they are connected to the coordinate plane! The x- and y-values help us know where to put the points on the plane from an equation.

Invite them to test this by picking a number of months less than 10. Ask them if this should be the x- or y-axis value. They should observe that it's the x-axis, because that's the number of months we are counting. Then they should see what y-value is in the corresponding point on the line. If they put the x-value back into their equation for the number of months, they should get the y-value as output. This can introduce writing a linear equation in slope-intercept form using x and y.

At this point, they should have the equation $y = 7x$. They should be able to extend this to the other line to write it in similar form: $y = 9x$. Ask them to find where the second line hits the 300 on the y-axis. They should see it's at around 33 months. With both lines on the graph, they can see the difference in months between the two lines, which is about 9 months.[4]

Another topic that patterns can be useful to introduce is number theory. Prime and composite numbers[5] are introduced in sixth grade. The traditional way to introduce them is through factor trees, greatest common multiple (GCM) and lowest common factor (LCF).

While there is nothing wrong with these understandings as far as they go, we can do better and go deeper. For example, prime and composite numbers can be introduced in younger grades, or to middle school students, with the book *You Can Count on Monsters* by Richard Schwartz.[6] This picture book uses drawings of monsters that are made up of elements based on the prime factors in each number; for example, the number 21 has a "7-monster" and a "3-monster" interacting. Numbers with more factors, like 12, have multiple prime factors interacting; 12 has two 2-monsters and a 3-monster.

Each of the monsters has its own recognizable image and personality. The facing page has diagrams and factor trees as well. With no words, students can extrapolate and discover a great deal about these factors and multiples while having fun. If time allows, an art connection can be that students design their own prime monsters and make their own composite monsters out of them. This would lead to a deep understanding of these patterns indeed.

Understanding factors and multiples can also be developed using manipulatives. For example, give students tiles or cubes and assign them a composite number, like 16. Have them make as many *arrays* with these manipulatives as they can, and record the result.[7] They should come up with a 1×16, 2×8, and 4×4 arrays. This is a fun activity to do in pairs, and the visible thinking there makes it easy for a teacher to circulate and ensure that the students are on task. This activity can also be done on paper, especially after students have experienced it with the manipulatives.

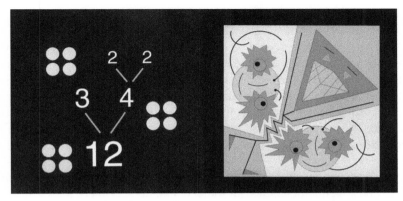

Figure 6.3. A side-by-side example of pages from the book. The left side shows the factor tree, and the right side shows the interaction between two 2-monsters and a 3-monster. Richard Evan Schwartz, *You Can Count on Monsters.*

Then in another class, when exploring volume of rectangular prisms, cubes can be pulled out again and students can explore how to make rectangular 3D shapes with different side lengths. For example, given 25 cubes, they can discover they can only make a rectangular shape in the dimensions of $5 \times 5 \times 1$ layer. This makes 25 a square number. Asked how many cubes they would need to make a perfect cube, they could play around or combine sets of cubes to see that it would need to be $5 \times 5 \times 5$, or 125 cubes—thus a cubic number. This also helps to open the door to exponential thinking.

Another great pattern exploration activity can be using a number chart to highlight patterns. One such activity by the author is available for free on Teachers Pay Teachers; in it, a chart is provided for students to fill in the counting patterns of the multiples.[8] On a basic level, such a chart can be used to recognize the connections between multiplication facts, as well as where square numbers appear, as a diagonal down the page.

But there is more: using colored transparent strips, equivalent fractions can be found by placing one on the numerator row and the other on the denominator row. For example, placing a strip on the top row of the chart that shows the number sequence $(1, 2, 3, \ldots, 12)$ and the other on the fourth row $(4, 8, 12, \ldots, 48)$ will show the student how one-fourth is equivalent to three-twelfths. More complex equivalents like the top row of threes and the bottom row of fifths can be used to find three-fifths, six-tenths, and so on. Experimenting with patterns like this can help students solidify their understanding of these equivalents, which can help with the standards of simplifying fractions and GCM/LCF in grade six.

INTRODUCING ALGEBRA

To Algebra I in middle school or not to Algebra I in middle school: that is the question. This has been at the center of many debates. Some teachers proclaim algebraic mastery among their charges at a young age; others assure us that students in general are in no way ready for these approaches and concepts. Still others say that the traditional high school pathway of Algebra I followed by geometry, Algebra II, trigonometry/precalculus, and calculus doesn't have enough time to complete unless students take Algebra I in eighth grade, so it's a must.

What does the research say? As a basic summary: "It depends." Some studies show better outcomes in some populations. Others show pushing Algebra I too quickly means shortcutting important foundations that mean students will have to repeat the subject matter they have already covered. In other words, just because they pass Algebra I in eighth grade doesn't mean they fully grasp the math. Many students who go through Algebra I in eighth

	1	2	3	4	5	6	7	8	9	10	11	12
1	1	2	3	4	5	6	7	8	9	10	11	12
2	2	4	6	8	10	12	14	16	18	20	22	24
3	3	6	9	12	15	18	21	24	27	30	33	36
4	4	8	12	16	20	24	28	32	36	40	44	48
5	5	10	15	20	25	30	35	40	45	50	55	60
6	6	12	18	24	30	36	42	48	54	60	66	72
7	7	14	21	28	35	42	49	56	63	70	77	84
8	8	16	24	32	40	48	56	64	72	80	88	96
9	9	18	27	36	45	54	63	72	81	90	99	108
10	10	20	30	40	50	60	70	80	90	100	110	120
11	11	22	33	44	55	66	77	88	99	110	121	132
12	12	24	36	48	60	72	84	96	108	120	132	144

Figure 6.4. A multiplication chart overlaid with colored strips to find equivalent fractions.

grade end up doing poorly in high school math and need to take remedial algebra again.

In fact, one longitudinal analysis shows that with the increase of higher-achieving students taking Algebra I in eighth grade, there is no corresponding increase in students taking more advanced math in later years. Another analysis shows that while higher-performing students may benefit, moderate- and lower-performing students often suffer from this acceleration. Why is this?

Something many people don't know about the way math education is structured to progress is that when the Common Core standards were written, algebraic concepts became integrated throughout the whole series of grade levels. From an early age, students should be encouraged to think of solving a math problem in terms of finding the unknown. If this is done well and thoroughly, when students reach algebra, they will be able to substitute a letter for the unknown and solve, applying the mathematical properties, such as commutative property, they are already well acquainted with. The increased rigor of the newer standards should lead to greater understanding and accomplishment in students.

In addition, the eighth-grade standards focus on many important mathematical concepts that are foundational for success in high school math. For example, the geometry in the grade eight standards makes proofs in high school more accessible. Transformations become intuitive because of the hands-on approaches. Learning about scientific notation and exponents makes exponent rules relatable.

There are explicitly algebraic concepts as well. For example, a major part of grade eight standards includes algebraic functions: what is a function, how to tell the difference between a function and a non-functional relation, linear functions, and more. These are topics traditionally covered in Algebra I anyway; providing conceptual and procedural exposure and practice in grade eight makes the work of Algebra I more achievable.

Having worked with many students who tackled Algebra I in eighth grade (or even seventh) because that is equivalent to "high achievement" in private or tracked schools, the author has seen the gaps appear firsthand and supported the struggles the students have experienced. These gaps caused some of them to stop liking or enjoying math.

One part of the disconnect is that while elementary and middle schools have been faster to adopt the revised standards and practices, many high schools have stayed firmly in the traditional approaches. Some have even stuck to old, procedural texts. Not only does this ignore the more rigorous and conceptual alignment of the whole Common Core progression, it also fails to make use of the great connections students could be making to prior work.

To illustrate, there is one wealthy district to which several families the author used to tutor moved in order to provide a better education to their children. To the author's surprise, some of the teaching was less effective than in other, poorer districts, especially in the accelerated classes. In these classes, the teacher would move very quickly and use traditional, procedural methods, leaving the burden of the learning on the students. Students with good memorization strategies or existing understanding would do well, but those who wanted or needed to truly understand would be left behind.

Even with tutoring, some students left the accelerated path to succeed better in the regular path. After doing so, and learning the concepts as well as the procedures, the students became independent and successful. These students are more likely to be able to retain and apply the mathematics they learned in life.

Like with the teaching of reading, as revealed in the podcast *Sold a Story*,[9] higher performance in these wealthy districts may not be due to better teaching; it may be better access to private tutors and programs that can close the gaps in the teaching.

In addition, having a calculus course as a goalpost may be a bit arbitrary; is it really necessary for all students before college? Yes, it plays a heavy role in college admissions. But is this justifiable? Engineering, marketing, medicine, architecture, and some other fields do use calculus. However, most fields, including many academic and professional fields, do not. In those fields, statistical analysis, modeling, applied mathematics, and/or data science may be more useful. Arguments could be made that financial literacy would be helpful for all.

Some states are revising their pathways in mathematics to de-emphasize the track toward calculus as the ultimate goal.[10] At the time of this book, there is a debate in California about a new framework being adopted that has some of the questions from this section at its center. The framework encourages focus on higher-order thinking, meaning-making, and problem solving, and it aims to make teaching more equitable. It also encourages studying data science in place of calculus, a move some university-level educators think is a mistake, though data science is a large and growing field.

What does all this point to? The opinion here is it's better to go slowly and thoroughly. With a vision toward the future, rather than seeing education as having a finite goal, it makes more sense to have a rigorous foundation that opens doors throughout the student's journey. This can help us reframe learning as a lifetime process, not a medal to achieve.

WORKING IN GROUPS

In chapter 5, we explored some structures and protocols for group work that facilitate student growth through peer work. While these are excellent for earlier grades, they are even more beneficial beginning in middle school.

As parents know, most children who previously looked to them for guidance and affirmation in all departments shift their focus to peers for approval and identity building in middle school. This change of focus away from adults and toward peers extends to the adult world in general; many adolescents look to the adult world as examples of exactly how they do *not* want to be. It's the rare teacher who can build trust and confidence with all their students. Many earn mockery or bland acceptance instead.

For educators who want students to grow instead of coasting through math, this change in focus can be leveraged toward that goal. Homeschooling parents can do this through finding peer groups their child can work with, either in person or remotely. Teachers can redirect the social energy toward growing skills that will serve the students in school and beyond.

Math conversation protocols are important to implement to support productive conversations in math class. Giving students a problem and telling them to discuss it will lead to spotty results if there is no other guidance. They may well end up talking about someone's crush or what the history teacher did last period. Therefore, introducing protocols, modeling, and monitoring student conversation will help students be successful in developing these higher-level discussion skills. The development of these skills will serve them well in the workplace and in life.

In addition to, or as part of, the various protocols introduced in chapter 5, middle school teachers may want to provide cards with sentence stems and starters to support student discussion. They can be used in homeschooling settings as well, for parents with one student or several. Examples of sentence stems and starters include:

- I noticed that _____.
- I wonder if _____.
- My strategy was _____.
- How did you find your solution?
- I disagree with that strategy/solution because _____.
- Can you prove that to me?
- I agree with your strategy/solution because _____.
- I think you made a mistake because _____.
- That was really interesting. I learned something from you.
- That makes sense because _____.

- I got lost in your explanation when you said _____.
- Can you please explain that another way?
- What if we tried _____?

Prompting students with these types of discussion frames and giving them opportunities to practice them will scaffold the conversations. With practice, they will be able to leave the scaffolds behind, like with any other scaffold. If the conversations wander or lose focus over time after a class has developed this skill, a teacher can reinstitute the prompts, cards, or requirements to frame the conversations this way, to help students return to these practices. As a good teacher knows, students need to practice routines periodically because the skills will deteriorate.

CALCULATOR USE

As will be discussed in chapter 7, one pitfall many middle schools fall into is too much calculator use too soon. What is appropriate calculator use, and when should it be introduced?

First of all, calculators are a tool that can be used well or not well. They can be great fun for games and exploration by younger children. Presenting students with open-ended tasks such as, "Find as many ways as you can to make the number 17" can lead to infinite exploration and discovery. Sharing the many ways can open children's eyes to how numbers can work.

The issue comes when students use them for everything from long multiplication to dividing ten by two. Not only is the latter slower on the calculator for most people, it leaves more room for error by entry. Encouraging students to extend the computation work they did in earlier grades and connect it to higher levels of math pays off in many ways.

A good rule of thumb is that if the task or computation requires more effort than the objective of the work, a calculator can be useful. For example, the New York State standards require knowing all square roots through 225 and all cube roots through 125 in grade eight.[11] Knowing these allows reasoning[12] when simplifying or calculating roots, such as $\sqrt{135}$. Since 135 is between 121 and 144, the root must be between 11 and 12.

Then, calling upon their knowledge of factors and multiples, the student can see that since 135 ends in 5, it must be a multiple of 5, and since the digits sum to 9, it must be a multiple of 9. Finding the factors, they may see that $135 = 9 \times 15 = 3 \times 3 \times 3 \times 5$. If simplifying, that means the only square number is 9, so 9 can be rooted and 3 extracted from the square root symbol, making the simplified version $3\sqrt{15}$. Since 15 is less than 16, the root of 15 would be less than but close to 4, and $3 \times 4 = 12$, so $3\sqrt{15}$ makes sense.

If a decimal approximation of $\sqrt{135}$ is needed, it is appropriate to use the calculator to find it, and the result is ~11.62. Having reasoned about the value in advance and knowing it should be between 11 and 12, the student can be confident about the answer given by the calculator.

Another appropriate use of the calculator is for long multiplication or division problems, after students have developed the skills by grade six, so that they are able to approximate and reason about their answers. Complex percentage and ratio problems can be helped by them as well. Similarly, experience and fluency with calculators will serve students well as they get into more advanced math and need to find statistical values, trigonometric ratios, graphs of functions, and calculus-related calculations like derivatives, integrals, or limits.

An important note here is that there are some students with special needs who need to use a calculator from an early age. These students may never develop number sense the way others do, so support here should be toward helping them reason about what the calculator tells them. In time, they may be able to give up the calculator in some areas—but that's for another book.[13]

Important Practices

- Use tasks, protocols, and technology to differentiate for different learners' ZPD.
- Help students to connect topics in math to life and existing knowledge to make them relevant.
- Use patterns to introduce a variety of topics:
  - Different bases and ways of counting
  - Algebraic sequences and graphs
  - Prime and composite numbers
  - Area and volume of rectangular shapes and prisms
  - Equivalent fractions
- Consider when it is best to introduce Algebra I developmentally to your student(s), and do so with proper supports.
- Use group work wisely and deliberately, scaffolding with discussion prompts.
- Consider carefully when and how to introduce calculators, and encourage students to use what they know about math operations before doing simple computations on one.

What was your greatest insight about math when you were in middle school?
The author loved learning that a variable just takes the place of a number or value we don't know yet.

NOTES

1. Salman Khan, *The One World Schoolhouse: Education Reimagined* (London: Hodder & Stoughton, 2012).

2. Find the activity at https://www.geogebra.org/m/wkdwZpY2.

3. The *domain* is the set of values that exist as a starting point for the data set; in this example, it's the number of months. The *range* is the output from the function, or the values we get when we enter each value from the domain. For example, month 10 at $7 per month would give us $70 as the output; if we stop at month 10, the range would be 70.

4. Solutions: $84 after 1 year; $300 ÷ 7 = 42.86 months, or 43 months, or 3 years 7 months; 300 ÷ 9 = 33⅓; 34 months; 2 years 10 months. The rate to save $300 at $9 per month is nine months faster than with $7 per month.

5. A prime number is a number with no factors other than itself and one. A composite number has multiple factors. For example, 11 is a prime number because its only factors are 11 and one. Twelve is composite because its factor pairs are one and 12, two and six, and three and four.

6. Richard Evan Schwartz, *You Can Count on Monsters: The First 100 Numbers and Their Characters* (Providence, RI: American Mathematical Society, 2015).

7. In this context, an *array* is shapes, objects, or drawings arranged in a rectangle divided into rows and columns with equal numbers in each. See also John A. Van de Walle, *Elementary School Mathematics: Teaching Developmentally*, 2nd ed. (New York: Longman, 1994).

8. Available under Resources on the author's website, susanmidlarsky.com.

9. *Sold a Story* podcast, American Public Media, 2022. Note that this podcast was instrumental in moving many schools toward the "science of reading." There is a similar push among a small group of educators toward the "science of math," though the two subjects have a very different teaching history.

10. See Charles A. Dana Center, *Launch Years: A New Vision for the Transition from High School to Postsecondary Mathematics* (Austin: University of Texas, 2020), https://www.utdanacenter.org/sites/default/files/2020-03/Launch-Years-A-New-Vision-report-March-2020.pdfhttps://utdanacenter.org/launchyears.

11. From NY-8.EE.2: "Know square roots of perfect squares up to 225 and cube roots of perfect cubes up to 125. Know that the square root of a non-perfect square is irrational."

12. Standard for Mathematical Practice 2: "Reason abstractly and quantitatively."

13. This refers to students with *dyscalculia*, a rare math disability.

Chapter 7

Fractions

Messy or Magical?

Before I worked with you, I hated fractions. Now they're my favorite!
—*Multiple students*

Mention the word *fractions* to anyone over the age of ten, and you tend to get a response on one extreme or the other. Typical responses include:

- I hate fractions!
- I never understood fractions.
- I love fractions!
- I'm an adult and never needed to use fractions. They should be removed from the curriculum.

The last was from an influential trainer on Twitter, a professional woman who started a crusade to take rigorous math out of school. She reached many receptive ears, because who wants to be burdened by an opaque and useless system when they can find other ways to accomplish necessary tasks in life?

On the other hand, perhaps she can manage her life without knowing fractions—but what is she missing? How does she know what her life would be like if she understood and was competent in using them?

As one's understanding of fractions grows, certain life tasks and understandings may become easier. For example, cooking can become far more intuitive. Being able to use the same measuring cup for multiple ingredients helps to cut down on dishes to wash and helps the environment in a small way. Understanding ratios and percentages allows everything from winterizing an RV effectively or adjusting a knitting pattern to calculating financial plans and budgets or planning a trip. These changes may not be earth shattering, but they relieve stress in life, and for those with big ambitions, they may enable bigger plans.

In an early workshop the author presented to fellow teachers, one teacher dissolved into unrelenting tears. The reason was because she was finally, in her late forties, understanding aspects of math that had been blocked from her comprehension. She realized that had she had access to these understandings earlier, she would have had a much easier life; she was grieving for what she had been missing.

To get the most out of this chapter, try your hand at this sixth-grade math problem.

In a flash mob event, participants are told to show up in a blue, red, yellow, or green shirt. Two-fifths of the participants come in blue, one-third in red, and the rest in green and yellow. The total number of red, green, and yellow shirts is 126. How many red shirts are there?

If you finish the previous problem, try this addition:

There are three-fourths as many green shirts as yellow ones. How many yellow shirts are there?

How did you do?

If you're like many adults who have tried this problem, you probably tried solving it with equations and algebraic formulas. If that wasn't comfortable, maybe you tried drawing representations of shirts. Maybe you found there were 42 shirts. Maybe you found that the number of shirts became fractional at a certain point, which didn't make sense.

Many students will try their hands in similar ways with problems like this, find an answer, and then stick with that answer without reasoning about it, ending up with fractional shirts. Many adults will catch that error and rethink it. That's the ideal; it's an element of Mathematical Practice 1, which is to make sense of problems and persevere in solving them. Part of this is making sense of the answer. In Mathematical Practice 3, "Construct viable arguments and critique the reasoning of others," students should practice justifying their own work as well as critiquing that of others.

Let's have a look at one way fractions can be made more visible. For this, we'll draw upon the Singapore bar model, or tape diagram, practice again. It's not intended to be the only way, but it has been effective for many people who struggle to visualize fractions, and most people weren't exposed to this in school. Here is a think-aloud in visual form about the process; for best results, follow along with Figure 7.1 as you read.

a. What am I counting? I'm counting shirts. The participants are wearing colored shirts. Let me draw a whole, long bar to represent the set of participants.

Colored Shirts

b.

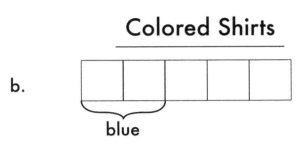

blue

c - g.

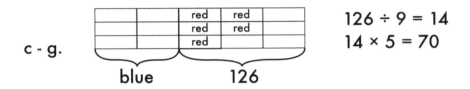

blue   126

$$126 \div 9 = 14$$
$$14 \times 5 = 70$$

i - j.

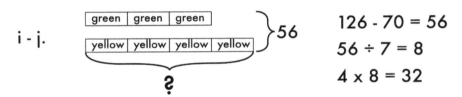

?

$$126 - 70 = 56$$
$$56 \div 7 = 8$$
$$4 \times 8 = 32$$

Figure 7.1. The models for solving the introductory word problem.

b. Okay, now it tells me two-fifths come in blue. So let me divide the bar into five, and I'll label two of the parts "blue."

c. Next it tells me one-third is in red. Wait a minute, how do I change fifths into thirds? I'm not quite sure, so I'll divide the whole thing horizontally into thirds as well. That looks like an area model, interesting!

d. How many parts are there in total now? Okay, it's 15. How many make a third? 5. Let me make 5 red.

e. Now it says the red, green, and yellow shirts are 126. That doesn't include the blue ones. So let me put a bracket around the red and the nonblue shirts now and show it as 126. How many parts does this include now?

f. Okay, it's 9 parts. And 126 is divisible by 9, because if I add the digits, I get 9 ($1 + 2 + 6 = 9$). I'm probably on the right track. And $126 \div 9 = 14$. So each part is 14.

g. I have 5 red parts that are worth 14 shirts each, so that's 5 × 14. I know 10 × 14 = 140, and 5 is half of 10, so if I cut 140 in half, I get 70. 70 red shirts.

h. Now let's look at the second part. I had ⁴/₁₅ left over as green and yellow. That's too hard to use to think about the next part, so I'll draw a new model.

i. For this one, I'll draw three bars labeled "green" above four bars labeled "yellow," since it's a comparison problem. That helps me visualize it. The total amount of shirts left over was 56. Let me indicate that with a label.

j. Now I have 7 parts, and 56 divides equally by 7, so that works. 56 ÷ 7 = 8, so each part is worth 8 shirts. Since there are four yellow bars, there are 32 yellow shirts.

I can use the numbers in my model to go back and check my thinking. I can even find out how many participants there were in all, and make sure the ⅖ works with blue, and there are no fractional shirts. 14 × 15 = (14 × 10) + (14 × 5) = 140 + 70 = 210. Two-fifths of 210. Well 210 ÷ 5 would be 21 × 2, or 42; double that (since 5 is half of 10, so the quotient would be double that of dividing by 10) would be 84. 84 + 126 = 210. It works!

Take a moment and reflect on this. What did you notice? Keep in mind that this is a sixth-grade problem, so the thinking relies on years of learning about fractions in elementary to be able to do this successfully.

ELEMENTARY PROGRESSION OF THE
CONCEPT OF FRACTIONS

What does the elementary progression that leads to success in the previous problem look like?[1]

In first grade, children should work with halves and quarters, with thirds introduced in second grade. This can be done using pattern blocks and a variety of different shapes, integrating geometry and fractions. In second grade, halves, quarters, and thirds relate to telling time on an analog clock.

Importantly, the language of units is kept, rather than symbols showing numerator and denominator. This helps to preserve the idea of fractions as something that can be counted, just like apples, hours, tens, ones, and so on. Therefore, we can count "one half, two halves," "one fifth, two fifths, three fifths, four fifths," and so on. This supports the idea of counting units, providing the basis for addition and subtraction of like units (denominators) in later grades.

Dr. Yeap Ban Har, an international expert and trainer in Singapore Math, provided the concept of fractions and decimal fractions as *nouns* in a training in January 2023.[2] He introduced the idea of counting nouns—in which apples, fractions, decimal values, and so on are all countable nouns. When students realize they can replace one noun with another, in combination with place value and number sense, math becomes more achievable.

This leads to grade three, in which the idea of the unit fraction is introduced. A unit fraction is one countable unit of a fractional size, such as one half, one fifth, and so on. After practicing with modeling and counting different fractional units, which can be done with paper folding, drawing, and/or fraction tiles, the conventional form of fraction writing, with numerator over denominator, can be introduced.

The number line is another important model; these can be made using fraction strips. In fact, find—or think of—a ruler. Can you see how it is a kind of number line with fractions on it? Depending on the markings and the measurements (metric or imperial, or both), these may be multiples of one-half, as the imperial system uses halves, fourths, eighths, and so on, or base-ten units, such as tenths, hundredths, and so on, on the metric ruler.

By now, with the idea of a fraction as a unit we can count being firmly embedded, it's the right time to introduce the complexity of writing fractions conventionally.

This is a good time to bring in a principle of teaching. When teaching new concepts, it's a good idea to introduce one complexity at a time. A mistake many teachers make is to introduce many complexities at once. For example, a word problem with new concepts might be introduced simultaneously with how to model them using bar models.

However, if the objective is to introduce, say, adding fractional units, it's better to introduce that first until students understand the concept, using our concrete-pictorial-abstract approach. On the other hand, if the objective is using bar models to solve problems about the addition of fractional units, it's best to introduce the word problems with simple fractions students can already manage. That way, students can be successful with one skill at a time, combining them later.

If you're wondering, "Why did this chapter start with a problem that combined many skills, then?" you are a critical thinker who is involved with the process! The reason for this choice is that as adults, many people think the way they learned math is best. The opening problem was chosen to illustrate that the methods of teaching in this book lead to ways of thinking that simplify complex problems and allow them to be achieved with less effort, making greater mathematical accomplishments possible.

Once third graders have a solid grasp of a fraction as a unit, the concept of a non-unit fraction can be developed. Third grade is also a year in which the concept of multiplication as multiple copies of a number is developed. This concept can be applied to fractions as well, where, for example, three-fourths is the same as three copies of one-fourth. This can be represented as ¼ + ¼ + ¼, or 3 × ¼.

One of the author's favorite activities is to give a set of fraction tiles, preferably the labeled plastic ones, to each student or pair of students, and allow students to simply explore and find out what they see. This invariably leads to discoveries that allow students to conceptualize properties of fractions, especially with perceptive teachers observing and guiding them. For example, for the student who starts to line up the one (whole) with full sets of halves, fourths, and so on, a question could be, "How many halves are the same as a whole? How many thirds? Maybe you can find out!" The student can then draw or journal their discovery and then share this with the class, if there is one, causing the whole class to progress.

Other possible guiding questions include:

- I notice you have a fourth lined up with two eighths. What other fractions are the same? What patterns do you notice in the numbers?
- How many thirds are the same as a whole? How many fourths? Let's write that down! Do you see a pattern in this?

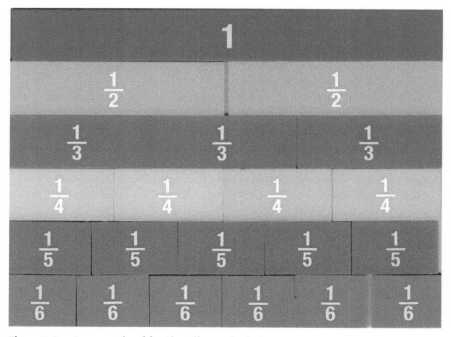

Figure 7.2.   An example of fraction tile manipulatives.

- Let's compare to a half. How many ways can you make equivalents to a half with different fraction tiles? Let's write those down as addition sentences. What patterns do you notice?
- Now a sixth. Which tiles can you make exactly the same length? Which can't you? What patterns do you notice? Let's write those down!
- What do you notice about the connection between the size of the pieces and the denominator?
- Use the patterns or constructions one student makes to prompt the others. Using a document camera or gathering others to look at the discovery can help students learn from each other.

By playing, writing, and questioning with the tiles, students can develop an instinctual and intuitive understanding of how unit and non-unit fractions work. They learn what "common denominator" means in relation to size of the fraction. This makes the common misconceptions about denominators easier to avoid.

Some common *misconceptions* include:

- Incorrectly believing that greater number in the denominator means the size is larger; for example, one-eighth is larger than one-fourth
- Incorrectly adding fractions by adding the numerators and denominators

As the students work with the tiles, they can learn about fractions in a way that helps avoid the misconceptions later in life. Questions like, "Why does a greater denominator mean smaller size pieces?" can help them reason about numerical value connections. Later, as they practice adding and subtracting fractions, drawing upon this experience ("Remember when we worked with the tiles?") can help them manage fractions fluently and catch and correct mistakes.

As always, the progression from concrete is followed by pictorial, or representational. Drawing models can help the students connect to their experience with the tiles. Historically, the favorite model was circles, like a pizza; however, cutting a circle is limited in its count and ease of drawing. Therefore, rectangular models are more useful for most concepts other than telling time. These also connect to both the area model and the bar model, as shown in the beginning of this chapter and explored more deeply later.

Another important concept is identifying the whole when considering a fraction. Take an index card and a piece of letter-sized paper, and fold them both in half. Unfold them, hold them side by side, and ask students which fractions they see. They should identify both as halves. A discussion about how they are different sizes despite both being the same fraction can ensue.

Then draw a rectangle with a line down the center. Shade the left half and half of the right half of the figure.

Ask students to identify the fraction. Some may say ¾; others may say one and a half. Without identifying what the whole is, it isn't possible to say. Pattern blocks can be helpful for these concepts as well; half of a hexagon is a trapezoid, but half of a parallelogram is a triangle, and so on. This is why labeling the whole on a fraction model is so important.

As students develop these understandings, the grade-four approaches to adding and subtracting fractions with like and unlike denominators can be linked to the previous understandings of like units, equivalent fractions, and factors and multiples. Traditionally, teachers have brought in lowest common denominator (LCD) and greatest common factor (GCF) when teaching these concepts. However, while factors, multiples, and prime and composite numbers are important concepts, LCD, GCF, and simplest form of a fraction aren't introduced until the grade six standards these days.

The reason for delaying these concepts is that focusing on these too early can lead to undercutting the concept. More examples will make this clearer. We can see this by exploring operations with fractions.

Grade three begins, and grade four continues, a lot of work with *benchmark fractions*, or fractions that allow easy mental estimation of value. Take, for example, the fraction one-half. If one is well versed in this fraction and its equivalents, it's easy to take on certain estimation tasks.

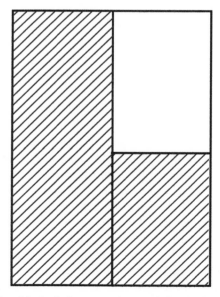

Figure 7.3.   Rectangle with shaded parts and an undefined whole.

Therefore, if students are well versed in the concept of "half," they will understand that three is half of six, four is half of eight, and so on. With that understanding, seeing fractions such as ³⁄₆, ⁴⁄₈, and so on, will automatically call up the equivalent concept of one-half. If a student with this understanding is asked whether ⁵⁄₆ or ⅓ is greater without computing, they will use their understanding of benchmark fractions to address this task. Since ⅓ is less than ½, and ⁵⁄₆ is greater than ³⁄₆, then ⁵⁄₆ must be greater than ⅓.

Students can visualize this concept with fractions models and number lines. They also work with benchmark fractions such as one-fourth, three-fourths, and so on.

Examples of tasks that would involve benchmark fractions include:

- Fraction comparison games[3]
- Asking students to order sets of fractions, such as ²⁄₅, ¹⁄₉, ⁵⁄₄, from greatest to least or least to greatest
- Asking students to place fractions on a number line using estimation of value

OPERATIONS USING FRACTIONS

When there is a thorough understanding of fractions and the concept of their value, how can we introduce operations, meaning addition, subtraction, multiplication, and division, with fractions? At the beginning of this chapter, we considered that most people don't grow up learning visual representations of fractions. However, a conversation with a teacher in China comes to mind.

The man had grown up in Singapore and was working in an international school. He had reverted to traditional methods of teaching the math, using formulas and memorization. When the author asked him why he wasn't using the modeling approach, he shrugged. We worked through several problems together, and his face lit up. He recalled these approaches and how much easier they made the math. He reflected that he didn't know why he had abandoned the way he had learned, and he resolved to use the approaches that had made his learning so much more fruitful in school.

The following pages outline a progression of how the operations are introduced in school, along with visual models that can be useful for learning them.

Addition

Let's start with adding one-third and two-fifths. This is one where we wouldn't find an LCD without multiplying the denominators, so it's a good one to begin with. Feel free to draw along with the descriptions to make it easier to understand what is being said.

We would either have a template with, or draw, two equal squares, at least 1.5 inches on each side to give enough space for drawing. First we would label both with a bracket and a "1," showing that each one represents a whole. Then on the first one, we would draw two lines vertically and shade one of the thirds, drawing a bracket with the fraction "⅓" beneath it. On the second, we would draw four lines within it horizontally, partitioning it into five equal parts. A strategy for this is to draw outside, outside, inside, inside to get fairly equal parts. We would shade two of the parts and label the fraction "⅖", like in Figure 7.4.

Now it's visually clear that the internal parts are not the same size, so we can't just add across. If working with a student or students, elicit ideas about how we can make them the same size. Either they will come up with it themselves, or you can suggest partitioning each square the same way as the other—that is, the first square gets four horizontal lines, and the second gets two vertical lines. No more shading is necessary.

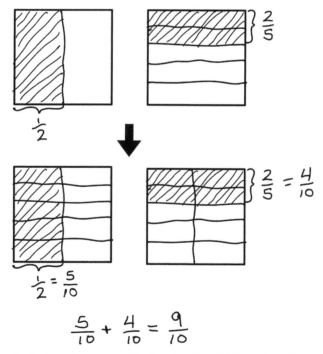

$$\frac{5}{10} + \frac{4}{10} = \frac{9}{10}$$

Figure 7.4.   Student work: area models showing the addition of two fractions.

Now we have made models with equal parts. How many total parts? How many shaded parts? Label the fractions with the new equivalent values: "$\frac{5}{15}$" on the first one and "$\frac{5}{15}$" on the second.

For students who need very explicit learning, a new model can be drawn where the parts from each model are taken and shaded in, perhaps in different colors, to show the sum. For others, it's enough to see that the parts can be added to make a sum of $\frac{11}{15}$.

What about situations where we would usually find the least common denominator? Let's say we want to add one-half and three-fifths. Traditionally, we would find the lowest common multiple of two and ten and make them both tenths. However, now we would start with a set of two area models and do the same thing to each one to make the model. Once we have the equal-sized units, we can add them to find the sum.

Students who are able to visualize and draw upon their understanding of equivalent fractions may realize right away that one-half is equivalent to five-tenths, so they can add five-tenths and three-tenths and get eight-tenths without any trouble. They may even realize that eight-tenths are equivalent to four-fifths. But these are not the students we worry about learning fractions! They are excellent students to call upon to share their thinking and strategies for the other students to learn more; however, we want to make fractions accessible and fun for all, which is why we use these visualization strategies.

Subtraction

A similar approach can be used for subtraction. This time, though, after we partition both models the same way and find the common unit, we look back at the first model and remove the quantity we found in the second model.

Take, for example, $\frac{1}{2} - \frac{1}{3}$. We can partition the first model in two vertically and the second model in three horizontally, remembering to label our whole and shade and label our fractions.

Next, we partition each model the same way as the other model: we add horizontal partitions to the first and a vertical partition to the second. Now we have one model with three sixths and one model with two sixths. A helpful strategy is to circle the first model to show this is the whole, or the *minuend*, and the only amount that we start with; the second model is to help us find out how much to take away. Now we can cross off two sixths from the first model and find that one sixth remains: $\frac{1}{2} - \frac{1}{3} - \frac{3}{6} - \frac{2}{6} = \frac{1}{6}$.

Repeated practice with this will help students connect to the concept that subtracting halves, sixths, twenty-thirds, or whatever, units is the same as subtracting any other common unit. The procedure becomes meaningful, so they can apply the process of finding common denominators and subtracting with meaning and visualization.

Multiplication

If students continue with these types of models for addition and subtraction, using them for area models for multiplication makes the understanding of multiplying fractions, an easier procedure, more fluid. If students learn multiplying fractions with the procedure only, they are less able to reason about the math and catch errors.

How would multiplying fractions look on an area model?

The concept is based on the idea of multiplication as multiple copies of a unit. Therefore, for example, $3 \times \frac{1}{5}$ is the same as three copies of a fifth, or three-fifths. Students practice with copies of a unit to make a non-unit fraction starting in third grade, including with manipulatives and pictures.

Then in fourth grade, we begin to teach the connection with multiplication to find fractions of a whole. For example, $\frac{1}{3} \times 6$ is the same as a third of six. Students can draw six units—circles, objects, a bar model, and so on—and then split them into three parts, where each part equals a third, or two: $\frac{1}{3} \times 6 -2$.

This can become more sophisticated with models. Let's say we have three cupcakes but four people who all want an equal share. Dividing three things into four parts can be messy when you don't understand fractions. Try dividing all three cupcakes into four parts, though, and it becomes obvious: you now have twelve equal parts, and each person gets three of the fourths, or three-fourths of a cupcake. This helps students make connections between fractions and division as well, especially if you use real food!

With lots of playing and exploring with fractions, a pattern can become obvious. When a whole number multiplies a proper fraction,[4] the product is greater; when a proper fraction multiplies a whole number, the product is lesser.

In fifth grade, we multiply fractions by fractions as well. This is where the area model serves as a useful model again. Let's start simply, with $\frac{1}{2} \times \frac{1}{2}$, or half of a half. The concept can be shown by taking a regular piece of paper and folding it in half, and then folding it in half again. The direction of the fold doesn't matter; in fact, it can be helpful to have two pieces of paper and do it two different ways. When we unfold the paper, we can see four equal parts.

Then we can draw an area model that reflects that. Draw a square; then partition it vertically down the middle. You should see halves. Next, draw another line horizontally across the square. Now fourths become apparent. Doing this after the paper folding in the same way shows the progression from concrete to pictorial.

Next, partition a new square vertically in half; then draw new horizontal lines vertically through each half. We see fourths again, but in a different orientation.

A good question for students now is, "Do the two types of fourths have equal areas?" One way to check this is to take the paper that was folded all vertically and cut out one of the fourths, and then cut that in half to make two pieces that should cover the area of one of the fourths on the other folded page.

Another way to check it is to draw. On the model with a horizontal and a vertical partition, shade one of the fourths. Then draw two more vertical partitions so the model now shows eighths, with two shaded. On the other model, draw a horizontal partition and then shade two of the eighths in the same quadrant as on the first model. At this point, discuss how we can see that two eighths are equivalent to one fourth.

Once the concept is developed, with more examples as necessary, multiplying fractions on the area model can be worked. This time, only one square or rectangle at a time is needed.

Let's take $\frac{1}{4} \times \frac{2}{3}$ as an example. First draw a bracket over the square with the number 1 to show the whole. Draw three vertical lines on the model to make fourths, and shade in a fourth, then draw a bracket below the section and label it "$\frac{1}{4}$." Using colored pencils or diagonal shading, shade the fourth in one color or one direction.

Next, partition the square horizontally with two lines into thirds. Shade all the way across the model in two of the parts in another color or opposite shading. There should be a section now where the shaded parts overlap. Label your two thirds.

At this point, inspect the model for the new number of total parts. Rewrite the fractions with the new denominator, twelfths. Students should see they now have three twelfths vertically and eight twelfths horizontally. When we look at the overlapping parts, we should see there are two double-shaded twelfths. The product is the double-shaded parts, or the two twelfths.

Now consider asking:

- What happened when we partitioned the model both ways?
- What does the shading represent?
- How did we get the new denominator? What does that represent?
- Is our product greater or lesser than our starting value? How do we know?
- Look at the problem again: $\frac{1}{4} \times \frac{2}{3}$. How does the product, $\frac{2}{12}$, relate to those numbers?

By noticing and reflecting, and practicing with multiple different problems, students will begin to make meaning out of what might otherwise have been a memorized, fluent, but meaningless procedure for them. Then they can start to generalize and apply these principles to real life, for example, if they have to lay out an area of a building, a garden, and so on.

Next, the question can be asked, "What happens if you multiply a proper fraction by another proper fraction, or by a fraction greater than one, also known as an improper fraction or a mixed number?"

Mixed Numbers

Mixed numbers can be handled the same way as proper fractions, except that we deal with models greater than a whole.

Traditionally, the first step of any operation with mixed numbers is to convert the mixed number into an improper fraction. While that can be useful, it can also lead to numbers that are hard to work with. Sometimes dealing with the whole and some parts is easier.

To add with mixed numbers, only the fractional pieces need to be converted to common denominators. For example, for $1\frac{1}{8} + 2\frac{3}{4}$, rather than converting everything to eighths ($\frac{9}{8} + \frac{22}{8} = \frac{31}{8}$), and then needing to simplify this to $3\frac{7}{8}$, try finding only the common denominators first. This gives $1\frac{1}{8} + 2\frac{6}{8}$, which is easy to add together—wholes together, giving 3, and fractions together, for $\frac{7}{8}$, giving $3\frac{7}{8}$ This is simpler and can be faster than having to make improper fractions, add them together, and then find the simpler form. This is shown visually in Figure 7.5.

If adding gives a fraction greater than one, there is another strategy for making a mixed number that can also help. With the sum $\frac{31}{8}$, for example, rather than dividing and subtracting, try decomposing the fraction into number bonds, like in Figure 7.6. Students can find $\frac{8}{8}$, or a whole in eighths, until they can find no more whole numbers, with $\frac{7}{8}$ left over. Since $\frac{8}{8}$ is equivalent

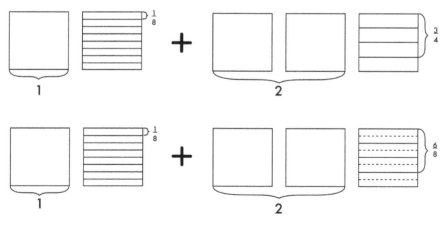

Figure 7.5.   Mixed number addition. The second set shows making a common denominator with the dashed lines.

to 1, the three $\frac{8}{8}$ make 3, so the mixed number is$3\frac{7}{8}$. Astute minds will see this is a repeated subtraction form of division, which is a useful concept to explore as well.

Similarly, we can decompose just one whole when subtracting from a mixed number. For example, take $2\frac{3}{8} - \frac{5}{8}$. Traditionally the procedure would be to turn the minuend into an improper fraction, $\frac{19}{8}$. In this case, instead of multiplying the whole by the denominator and then adding the numerators, making an improper fraction may make more sense by taking each of the ones in the whole number and making the equivalent one fraction ($\frac{8}{8}$), then adding the three fractions together ($\frac{8}{8} + \frac{8}{8} + \frac{3}{8}$), making $\frac{19}{8}$.

However, once we subtract $\frac{5}{8}$, we still have an improper fraction, $\frac{14}{8}$, which needs to be turned into a mixed number. Each of these steps is an opportunity for errors or misconceptions to creep in. Simplifying the process and connecting it to understanding can help with accuracy and success.

At this point, instead of converting the whole mixed number into an improper fraction, try decomposing only one of the whole numbers. This would look like changing $2\frac{3}{8}$ into $1\frac{11}{8}$. Then we can easily subtract $\frac{5}{8}$ from only the $\frac{11}{8}$, leaving $1\frac{5}{8}$ as the difference without having to do any additional conversions. Drawing models can show how this works and how only one model of a whole needs to be converted into fractional parts to have enough to take away.

Similarly, when subtracting a mixed number from a mixed number, making them into improper fractions is possible but not necessary. Take, for example $12\frac{2}{5} - 3\frac{4}{5}$. Instead of $\frac{62}{5} - \frac{19}{5}$, which may be challenging to subtract and then simplify, try subtracting the whole numbers first: 12 – 3 – 9. This leaves

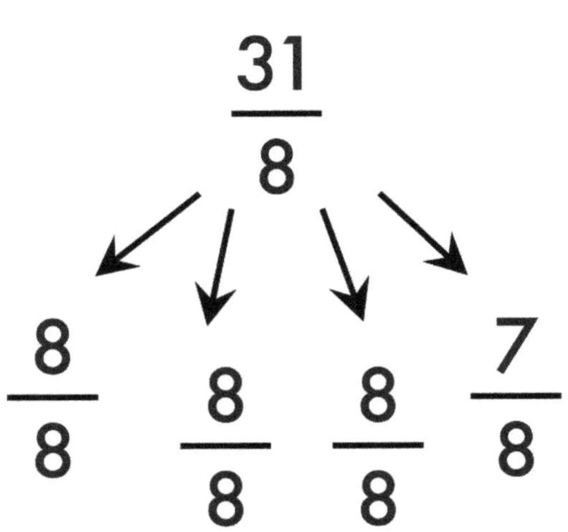

Figure 7.6. An improper fraction decomposed using number bonds.

$9\frac{2}{5} - \frac{4}{5}$, making it easy to decompose a whole from the minuend ($8\frac{7}{5}$) and subtract the $\frac{4}{5}$ from that, giving $8\frac{3}{5}$ as the difference, like in Figure 7.7.

Why does this work? It begins with the understanding of any number being a sum of smaller parts. Draw 13 separate square boxes. Partition one into fifths and shade and label two of the fifths, and draw a bracket under the remaining boxes, labeling them with the number 12. Now look at the diagram and think about taking away $3\frac{4}{5}$. Clearly we need more fifths, but we don't have to get them right away. We can take away the three wholes first. And look, we have $9\frac{2}{5}$ left, like in the previous paragraph! Now we can partition one of the whole squares into fifths as well and shade and label the $\frac{5}{5}$. This means we have $8\frac{7}{5}$ from which we can take away $\frac{4}{5}$, leaving $8\frac{3}{5}$ as our difference.

Another model to understand this is the flexible number line. Let's return to whole-number subtraction for this with the problem 42 − 29. Draw a

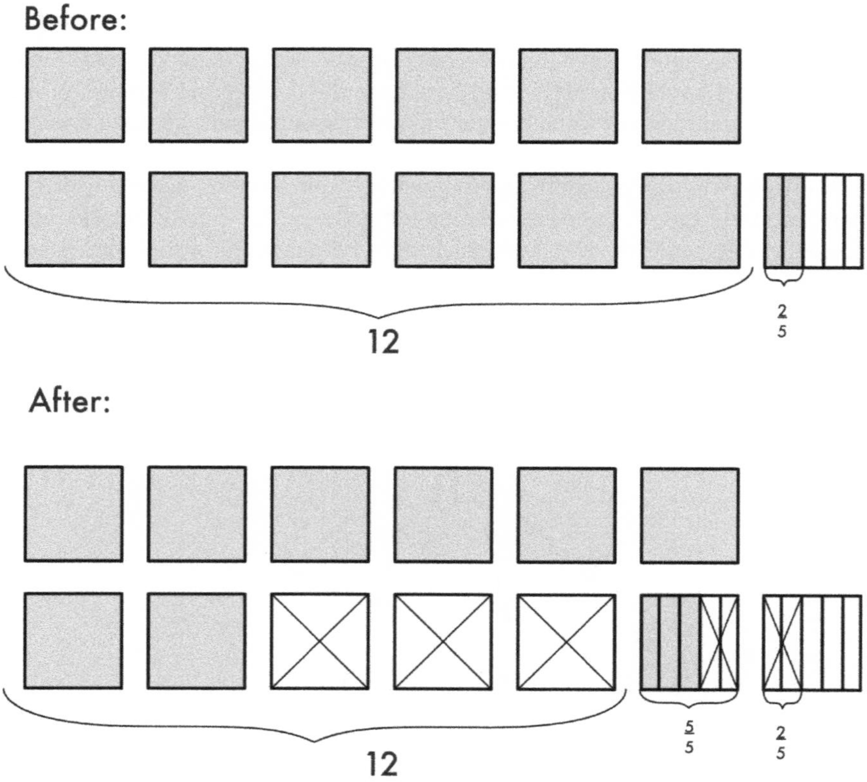

Figure 7.7. Subtracting a mixed number, showing models before and after decomposing one of the wholes and then subtracting.

number line and put the number 42 somewhere on the right. Now draw a jump backward by whatever number works for you. This example will use 20. $42 - 20 = 22$, so write 22 under the line to show that's where we landed.

We have 9 left of our 29 to go. Using what we know, we can decompose the 9 however it's easiest. Let's try going back two to start. Now we're at 20; let's record that.

Finally we have seven left. $20 - 7$ is 13; we can record this final jump on the number line. Looking back at our jumps, we can add them together to ensure that the sum is the *subtrahend*: $7 + 2 + 20$ is indeed 29. So our difference is 13.

Using the same understanding of partial differences, this also works for subtracting the mixed numbers, like in Figure 7.8. In the previous example, we began with 12⅖. We jumped back three to get to 9⅖. Here we can decompose a little differently as well. To take away ⅘, it's possible to break that into ⅖ and ⅖; taking away ⅖, we get to 9, and taking away another ⅖ (by breaking a whole into fifths), we get to 8⅗.

Even if one of these methods, including the traditional procedures, works best for someone, using the others when desired can allow for mental or written checks for accuracy.

When multiplying mixed numbers, the area model can come in extremely handy. Let's take, for example, $3⅔ \times 2¼$. Looking at each mixed number as a sum rather than as an entity, we can treat it like a binomial and use the distributive property.

Let's decompose the fractions into wholes and parts. We draw a rectangle wider than it is high to mirror its value. We write "3" across the top, draw a line starting most of the way across the top, and then write "⅔" over the remaining segment.

Next, we go to the left side and write a "2" to the left of the top part of the rectangle. Below that, we draw a line most of the way down horizontally across the rectangle and write "¼" to the left of that new segment.

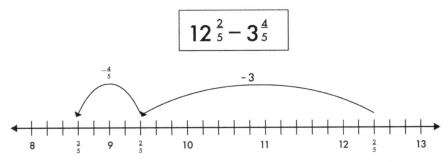

Figure 7.8. **Subtracting a mixed number using a number line and partial differences.**

Now we should have a rectangle with four segments. We use the concept of area to find the value of each rectangle. $3 \times 2 = 6$; we write "6" in that big rectangle. Going across, we have $2 \times \frac{2}{3}$, which is $\frac{4}{3}$, or $1\frac{1}{3}$. Write that in the top right rectangle. The lower left quadrant is $3 \times \frac{1}{4}$, which is $\frac{3}{4}$; finally, the last computation is $\frac{2}{3} \times \frac{1}{4}$, which is $\frac{2}{12}$.

Then we add all the products: $6 + 1\frac{1}{3} + \frac{3}{4} + \frac{2}{12}$. We can add the whole numbers first, making 7, and then make our fractions into common units: $\frac{4}{12} + \frac{9}{12} + \frac{2}{12}$. Leaving the last fraction in twelfths, in this case, made it easier to see the least common multiple for the common denominator. The sum of the fractions is $\frac{15}{12}$, or $1\frac{3}{12}$, which we can add to the 7 to make $8\frac{3}{12}$, or $8\frac{1}{4}$.

Division

Like with so many things, we are saving the best for last!

Dividing fractions is a challenge to so many people, mostly because they are just taught "keep-change-flip" and not how or why inverting the second fraction works for dividing. So let's back up and review some more effective ways of teaching the concepts.

In grade five, dividing a whole number by a fraction is introduced by the concept of *fitting*. What does this mean? To understand this, we need to step back to look at what division means.

If we look at division in general, there are two ways to see it: *partitive* division, or how many are in each part after you divide into parts; and *quotative* division, or how many groups there are when you know how many there are in each part.

For example, a partitive division question might be:

If you have 12 candies to share between 3 people, how many candies does each person get?

A related quotative division question might be:

If you have 22 candies and want each person to get 3 candies, what's the maximum number of people who can get candies?

With this example, you can see that while you can do 22 divided by 3, you can also see how many times 3 fits into 22, and how many are left over.

This kind of thinking can help us get started in the domain of fractions using division. Take, for example, a recipe that calls for four cups of flour, but your only cup measure is one-third of a cup. How many of these scoops will you need?

When we think about the fact that it takes three one-third cups to make a whole cup, or $3 \times \frac{1}{3} = 1$, it becomes intuitive to realize we will need four times that many to make our recipe: 3 one-third cups $\times 4 = 12$ one-third cups, so 4 cups $\div \frac{1}{3}$ cups $= 12$.

Here's another example. How many quarter hours are there in three hours: $3 \div \frac{1}{4}$? Again, we know there are four fourths in one hour. Using that fact, we can scale to any number of hours. Since we have three hours, $3 \div \frac{1}{4}$ hour $= 3 \times 4$ quarter hours $= 12$ quarter hours.

In both of these examples, $4 \div \frac{1}{3}$ and $3 \div \frac{1}{4}$, our result was 12. The same answer as if we inverted and multiplied, or 4×3 or 3×4! What an interesting pattern to explore.

Here we can see that there is more meaning developing than teaching students to "keep-change-flip." Over and over, teachers see that teaching that mnemonic, also known as KCF or related initials, lead to students making mistakes by "flipping" the wrong fraction or getting a quotient that doesn't make sense. When there is no meaning attached to mathematical teaching, students don't understand or realize their mistakes or how to correct them.

This recently happened in a fifth-grade classroom. The teacher, an eager learner but one who admits she is steeped in traditional ways of teaching, heard the advice about KCF but chose to disregard it, convinced that her students were doing well with the mnemonic. When the author was visiting her class, a student solved a fraction division problem on the board and inverted the first fraction, not the second, leading to an incorrect solution. This looked like $5 \div \frac{1}{3}$, but instead the student turned the dividend into $\frac{5}{1}$ and then inverted it, so it became $\frac{1}{5} \times \frac{1}{3}$, resulting in $\frac{1}{15}$. The correct solution would be $5 \times 3 = 15$. The teacher was entertained by the fact that she was disproved in front of the consultant about the very advice she had been given.

A different group shared that they found the fraction models for dividing fractions very useful. They became proficient at reasoning about fraction division using the models, and some were able to visualize the math without needing to draw them after some practice.

What would a model for dividing fractions look like?

Let's start with dividing a fraction by a whole number, $\frac{1}{2} \div 4$. That is, how many times does four fit into one-half?

Start by drawing a bar, labeling it to show the whole, and then cutting it in half and labeling the half. You can shade it as well if you prefer; an example is given in Figure 7.9.

Then split the half into four parts. Also split the other half into four parts so we can see the total number of parts in the model, which gives the size of the parts, or the denominator.

Since we are paying attention to the half we labeled, we need to see what the quotient is. Each one of the parts we split the half into becomes a quotient, because using the sharing definition of division, we are left with equal groups. Label one of these groups. Since the group number is one, and the size of it is an eighth, the quotient is $\frac{1}{8}$.

Let's try another one: ⅓ ÷ 2. Draw your bar, label your whole and your third, and then split each third into two. How many total parts? Six. How many labeled parts? One. The quotient is ⅙. Another way to say this is, "Two one-sixths fit into one third."

With a non-unit fraction, it can become easier or more complex. If we started with ⅔ and divided that by two, the quotient is just ⅓, because dividing by two is the same as cutting in half. In this case, connecting back to the understanding of a non-unit fraction as a sum of unit fractions helps us see that we are dealing with two units of a third, and we just cut those in half to find one of the units.

On the other hand, if we have a numerator that isn't easily divided by the divisor, it can be more challenging. Take ¾ ÷ 2. Since three is an odd number, we can't just split it in half. How many times does 2 fit into ¾? The answer must be fractional, because 2 is greater than ¾.

To develop the concept, let's back up to ¾ ÷ 1. Imagine we didn't know the identity property of division and that the result will be the same as the dividend. Draw two bars, labeling one "1." On the other, partition into four parts and shade three of them; label this one "¾." How much of the one-bar fits into the three-fourths bar? Yes, three-fourths of it!

We can extend this to ¾ ÷ 2. Since 2 is double 1, the quotient must be half the size. If this doesn't make sense, compare 8 ÷ 2 and 8 ÷ 4. The quotient of the second, with double the divisor, is half the quotient of the first. Try this out with other division examples until it makes sense. Then ask, what is half of ¾? Draw a horizontal line in your model to split it in half, and double-shade the top parts. The new fraction is ⅜.

Let's compare this to "invert and multiply." If we multiply ¾ × ½, which is the "invert-and-multiply" version of the fraction division, we can see that indeed, the product is ⅜: the same as the quotient when we approached the same problem as a conceptual division problem.

What about dividing a fraction by a fraction? To explore the concept of division by fitting, let's try a simple example: ½ × ⅛. Look at the models of ½ and ⅛ in Figure 7.9. How many copies of ⅛ fit into the ½? That's right, 4! The same result as if we did ½ × ⁸⁄₁.

If your brain is tired at this point, you'll see why so many teachers and students want to revert to the procedural routines. As we discussed, that might be fine in the short term. However, a bit more effort in learning means longer retention possibility. Perseverance is the key—remember the importance of "not yet!"

So far, we've reviewed the four operations with fractions and how to approach them conceptually, making connections from that to the procedures. What happens with fractions after fifth and sixth grade?

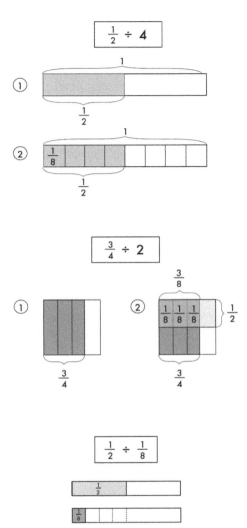

Figure 7.9. Models for dividing fractions.

FRACTIONS IN HIGHER GRADES

Starting in sixth grade, students can use their solid understanding of fractions to approach percentages. In the first place, understanding decimal numbers as *decimal fractions*, or fractions with a denominator that is a multiple of ten, allows students to extend their knowledge of place value and connect this to fractions and equivalent fractions.

Take, for example, 48%. This is the same as $^{48}/_{100}$. When the number is placed on a place value chart, it becomes obvious that it's also 0.48. To visualize this, draw a square and break it into 100 squares by partitioning it by ten both horizontally and vertically, and labeling the square as "1." Then color or shade 48 of the squares. This shows the value of $^{48}/_{100}$ relative to a whole, and why 48% is less than one.

One fun fact about the percent sign is it's kind of like a 100 with the one placed diagonally between the two zeros. This can be a visual reminder for students who forget that "percent" means "out of 100," so they can write the percentage as a fraction out of 100 and go from there.[5]

Sometimes when students are stuck when trying to move between three equivalent representations, that is, fraction, decimal, and percent, they can be encouraged to speak aloud the place value and use that to understand the concept. This is one reason it's important to encourage students to read decimal fractions with place value and not just, for example, "point four eight." If they can read 0.48 as "forty-eight hundredths," that can prompt them to write $^{48}/_{100}$, which can then lead to the connection to 48%.

Fluency with equivalent fractions, the work that begins at grade four, can make finding percentages simple as well. For example, seeing a denominator of ten makes finding a denominator easy by just multiplying both numerator and denominator by ten, mentally: $^{3}/_{10} \times {}^{10}/_{10} = {}^{30}/_{100}$. Likewise, the other factors of 100, such as 4, 5, 10, 20, 25, 50, and so on, can be multiplied, and multiples of 100, such as 200, 300, 1000, and so on, can be divided. Thus, and $^{3}/_{200} \div {}^{2}/_{2} = {}^{1.5}/_{100} = 1.5\%$.

Finding more challenging conversions can be done using this strategy as well. For example, say the task is to convert $^{5}/_{8}$ to a percentage. Since 8 is not a factor of 100, but 4 is, we can change the denominator to 4 by dividing. Then we use decimal numerators for the percentage value and the distributive property for mental multiplication. Thus, $^{5}/_{8} \div {}^{2}/_{2} = {}^{2.5}/_{4}$. Following that,

$$\frac{2.5}{4} \times \frac{25}{25} = \frac{(2 \times 25) + (0.5 \times 25)}{100} = \frac{50 + 12.5}{100} = \frac{62.5}{100} = 62.5\%.$$

With time and practice, this can be come mental math performed on the spot!

For more challenging percentages with no related factors to 100, we can solve using an algebraic setup, keeping in mind we are always finding equivalent fractions. Take $^{3}/_{7}$. Since we are trying to make it into a fraction over 100, we can set up the equation $^{3}/_{7} = {}^{n}/_{100}$, where n will be the value of the percentage.

We can then multiply both sides by the value of both denominators to eliminate the denominators and keep the value the same: $100 \times 7 \times {}^{3}/_{7} = {}^{n}/_{100} \times 100 \times 7$. Then we have $700 \times {}^{3}/_{7} = {}^{n}/_{100} \times 700$. Eliminating the common factors by dividing, a.k.a. "simplifying" or "canceling," we get $100 \times 3 = n \times 7$, or $300 = 7n$. Dividing both sides by 7, we get ~42.86%. Does this make sense? Well, since 3 is a little less than half of 7, and 43% is a little less than half, then yes it does!

Drawing models other than the area model can help too. A place value chart with decimal, fraction, and percent representations can be helpful. So can a bar model or double number line. A bar model split into parts can be used as a kind of "percentage ruler," helping students find a percentage of a quantity more easily, like in Figure 7.10. For example, finding 20% of 84 can be done by splitting a bar into 10 parts, labeling the whole as 84, and then finding what 10% (or one-tenth) of 84 is first. Then 8.4 can be written in one or more of the parts, since they are all the same size. Because 20% is just two sets of 10%, doubling 8.4 makes finding 20% easy.

This can be extended to multiples of five as well. Finding 25% of 84 can be done using the same percentage ruler but subdividing the third unit into two parts. With each smaller part now worth 4.2, it's a simple matter of adding 8.4, 8.4, and 4.2 to find 25%. Alternatively, the student may choose to partition the whole bar into four, since 25% is equivalent to one-fourth, and divide 84 that way.

A double number line can be used to model the same process. The advantage of this is that it's possible to mark the progression of value. Where in a bar model, each part should be marked by its corresponding quantity, a double number line can show increasing values.

A double number line is a useful representation for working with ratios as well, which is a major focus in grade six, leading to the understanding of proportionality in grade seven. Both this model and the bar model can simplify ratios and rates, which are both additional expressions of fractions, for ease of conceptual understanding and working. Many people find ratios much easier to compute mentally with these visual representations.

Ratios and rates are two of the most useful concepts in adult life, along with percentages. For example, understanding one's vehicle's mileage per

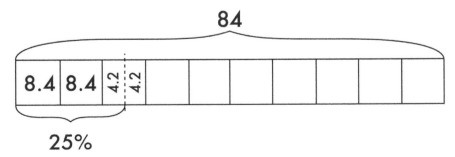

Figure 7.10. A percentage ruler used to find 25% of a quantity.

gallon can help one plan a trip and budget for fuel, as well as plan whether or not to stop at this gas station, or wait. Doubling and halving recipes are within the grasp of most people if the recipes have whole-number measurements, but this can be challenging if they don't. In addition, what if you're making rice in a cooker that calls for $1\frac{1}{4}$ cup of water for each cup of rice, but you only have $\frac{2}{3}$ cup of rice left? Guessing the water quantity could lead to burned or mushy rice. Fluency with unit rate can help with this.

In the rice example, one way to approach this is to look at it through unit rate. The ratio of rice to water is $1{:}1\frac{1}{4}$. What, then, is $\frac{2}{3}$ cup of rice worth? We can use tables, double number lines, or an algebraic approach. Note that we are keeping measurements fractional because that is how most cup measures work.

- This is a table that also breaks down a way to look at it mentally:

Rice (cups)	Water (cups)
1	$1\frac{1}{4}$
$\frac{1}{2}$	$1\frac{1}{4} \div 2 = \frac{1}{2} + \frac{1}{8} = \frac{5}{8}$
$\frac{1}{3}$	$1\frac{1}{4} \div 3 = \frac{1}{3} + 1/12 = 5/12$
$\frac{2}{3}$	$5/12 \times 2 = 10/12 = 5/6$

- Algebraic solution:

$$\frac{1}{1\frac{1}{4}} = \frac{\frac{2}{3}}{w}$$

What is this? It's a complex fraction! These are introduced in grade seven. They can also be rewritten as division expressions: $1 \div 1\frac{1}{4} = \frac{2}{3} \div w$. Using invert and multiply, we make the mixed number into an improper fraction $\frac{5}{4}$, and then invert it. The computation now becomes $1 \times \frac{4}{5} = \frac{2}{36} \times \frac{1}{w}$.

Multiplying to simplify, we get $\frac{4}{5} = \frac{2}{3w}$. To solve for w, we can multiply both sides by $3w$, since the right side has $3w$ in the denominator. That gives us $3w \times \frac{4}{5} = \frac{2}{3w} \times 3w$. Multiplying, we get $\frac{12w}{5} = 2$. Now multiply both sides by $\frac{5}{12}$ to isolate the variable: $\frac{5}{12} \times \frac{12w}{5} = 2 \times \frac{5}{12}$. Multiplying one more time, we achieve our result: $w = \frac{10}{12} = \frac{5}{6}$.

Phew! That was a lot of steps. With practice and understanding, it's possible to reduce the steps and do several at once, but it was important here to draw out the thinking, rather than encouraging procedural shortcuts such as "cross-multiplying" or "the butterfly method," which often lead to wrong applications and solutions due to lack of understanding.

One challenge schools often meet is that once students reach middle school, they are handed a calculator and told to solve problems with that. Not only does that cause the conceptual computation understanding they have developed thus far to atrophy, it also undercuts their ability to make sense of the math and reason about it. In addition, when they reach higher-level math that involves computation and problem solving with algebraic functions and equations that involve fractions, they can get lost.

A simple example of this is applying fraction understanding to graphing the slope of a linear function. Take the function $y = \frac{3}{5}x + 16$. If students are asked to graph this, and they understand the meaning of the function—including that the slope is the differences in the y-values over the differences in the x-values—they will know to put a point at (0, 16).

From there, they can travel three up and five over to graph subsequent points, or three down and five backward to continue the line into the second quadrant. Turning $\frac{3}{5}$ into 0.6 doesn't make this process as transparent.

Another example of where understanding fractions is important is in working with trigonometric ratios. Many people use SOH-CAH-TOA, which is a useful mnemonic because it doesn't lead to misconceptions. SOH, for instance, means that the *sine* of an angle is equal to the ratio of the opposite side from the angle *over* the hypotenuse, which makes a fraction.

While this computation could be done using a calculator, the sense-making is more effective if the student has a sense of fraction value. That is, if the opposite side is 13 and the hypotenuse is 22, the student should realize they made a mistake if they get a value greater than 1 or very small; instead, it should be close to one-half. Perhaps they divided the hypotenuse by the opposite side, or perhaps they forgot to enter the 3 in the number 13. Good fraction number sense allows for success in all these departments.

Important Practices

- Have manipulatives such as fraction tiles on hand throughout the introduction of new fraction concepts and fraction operations.
- Explore fraction concepts and operations using models before introducing procedural approaches.
- Avoid shortcuts like "keep-change-flip" or the butterfly method.
- Avoid encouraging calculator use too soon or for the wrong purposes.

What is an area in your life where a better understanding of fractions would serve you well?

The author has seen benefits from this in financial planning, especially in investments and interest rates.

NOTES

1. The *Progressions for the Common Core State Standards* document provides guidance for how learning ideally progresses from grade to grade in each math subject area. See Common Core Standards Writing Team, *Progressions for the Common Core State Standards for Mathematics* (Tucson: Institute for Mathematics and Education, University of Arizona, 2022), https://mathematicalmusings.org/wp-content/uploads/2023/02/Progressions.pdf.

2. Mathodology Roundtable, January 24, 2023, https://vimeo.com/792266165.

3. Find one such game for free at http://tasks.illustrativemathematics.org/content-standards/3/NF/A/3/tasks/2108.

4. A note about proper and improper fractions: The word *proper* refers to the definition of a fraction having a numerator lesser than the denominator. Therefore, an improper fraction is one with a numerator that is greater than the denominator. It has nothing to do with moral propriety. It can be helpful to discuss this with students when introducing precise mathematical vocabulary.

5. View an animation showing this at https://susanmidlarsky.com/animated-percent-symbol/.

Chapter 8

High School

Success or Failure

At this point in time, a strong foundation in math concepts can lead to successful tackling of the more technical math in high school. Alternatively, if students fell off the intended line of learning, they could have growing gaps that can lead to feelings of failure. In this chapter, we'll look at the outcomes of both of these stories and what we can do to help those with gaps. Some of it will be a bit technical, but with a bit of perseverance, it will become clear.

DIVERGING PATHWAYS

By the time students reach high school, they either have developed a strong, successful foundation, or they haven't. At this point, if we picture math development as a graph, a student could either have a climbing line of understanding, or if the learning was interrupted, there could be a plateau or even a falling line. Each of these situations leads to very different outcomes.

Let's look at a few stories of students of average intelligence. Imogene was taken out of school in fourth grade for health reasons. She missed two full years of school while she was hospitalized and recovering her health. However, her mindset was that she was capable, so when she returned to school, she worked hard to regain lost ground. Her family hired some outside tutors to help her close gaps in her math education. With support, she was able to complete the full course of high school math and feel good about it. Her chosen career, marketing, required learning calculus, which she was able to study and understand. Now she lives and works on her own and uses math competently in her daily life.

On the other hand, Joseph went to schools where he was taught rote procedures. He did well at first, in elementary school, but as math got progressively more abstract, he couldn't keep up. Math felt like a bunch of encrypted codes to him, where the teacher understood the language but it was a mystery to him. He tried to seek help, but his parents disliked math and couldn't help him understand it. Additional help from his school came in the same approaches, with more memorization and explanation of rules about how it worked, not why. He became convinced that he was just not a math person, like his parents. He continued through school in remedial classes, not caring about math or trying any more beyond the minimum to graduate.

After school, he relied on calculators and didn't realize when he made mistakes. He had to hire professionals to do his math for him, such as on his taxes. He racked up credit card debt and was bewildered by how it became so massive so quickly. He had trouble saving money and avoided any job or career that required him to use math. He also had trouble when life brought him problems to solve; he became stressed and anxious, and he was more easily misled when presented with false information.

A third student started school at a private school where he was taught the way this book suggests, by concepts before procedures and at a pace that worked for him. While there was only about half an hour in the day to study math, he made good progress, but he was average for the class.

After a couple of years, financial obstacles caused his parents to move him to the local public school. Where he had been average in math in the small private school, he was so advanced in the public school, where they spent an hour and a half on math each day, that they kept accelerating him higher, but they weren't able to challenge him appropriately. Eventually, this and other factors caused his parents to find a way to move him back to the private school. He continued doing well and strengthening his problem-solving abilities. He was able to manage well when the private school closed and he returned to public school. His strong foundation in math led him to excel in school and win awards and a membership in the National Honor Society, as well as admission to a competitive university and a major in economics.

It's easy to recognize trends in oneself in any of these young people. Most people are not in one extreme or another. Those on greater extremes of aptitude will generally have more extreme learning outcomes as well. However, with the right approaches, we can reach all students.

Looking back at middle school and the discussion about algebra, if a student is accelerated into algebra in grade eight, they will generally start in geometry in grade nine. This can be a turning point for the students. If they had a strong enough foundation before this, they can generally proceed smoothly. However, the eighth-grade standards include a lot of areas that lead to success in geometry; without these, geometry can be a huge challenge, especially if the focus is mostly on proofs. Solving for angle measures also requires competency in algebra.

Therefore, if the student mostly skipped the eighth-grade content and went straight to algebra, they may or may not succeed at this point. Mindset is a big part of this; if they believe they can do it and just have gaps in understanding, they will seek the practice and concepts that will allow them to construct the missing parts. However, if they have been frustrated for too long or given to believe they don't have the capacity, this can be the inflection point where they begin to fail. They may drop geometry, if given the opportunity, and retake algebra. Then they may see themselves as a "slow track" person and again, think they are "not a math person."

One story illustrates this. A friend, let's call him Abel, who generally struggled in math, did very well on a math exam. His teacher, rather than encouraging him to build on that success, told him that it was pure luck and that he "wasn't a math person anyway." The teacher didn't do this out of spite; he thought he was encouraging Abel to manage his expectations and not get his hopes up about math success.

Another way to look at this is that Abel could have made a developmental breakthrough and finally been able to excel at math. He could have made a leap with new confidence that with the right kind of work, he could "be a math person." In fact, his father had excelled in math; even from a fixed mindset perspective, meaning the belief that math ability is inherited, Abel should have been encouraged. Instead, the few words of the teacher had a weighty impact on Abel and his self-image, as well as the paths he pursued in life.

If students go at a pace that makes sense for them, they will still be at the mercy of the teaching style of the high school math teachers. While there are many stellar teachers in high school, there are those people who majored in math education because they found math intuitive, so they have a hard time teaching students who learn differently from their way of learning. The burden of the learning, therefore, is placed on the students; if they don't learn, it's because the students are lazy and incapable, not because the teacher failed to reach them.

ADDRESSING THE ISSUES

How can we overcome some of these obstacles?

First, relying on scores and reports from previous grade levels may not provide the insight we need into the levels the students can achieve currently. With the issues of temporary learning that have been discussed previously, a high score on an exam last month may not represent mastery today. How can we tell where students' capabilities actually lie?

One strategy to help with this is using benchmark assessments. This means, when students start a new grade level or topic, it can be helpful to give a preassessment to mark the starting point of their knowledge. This can reveal gaps or previous mastery, making the learning less scattershot and more targeted to actual student needs. If we don't take account of the gaps, we could be teaching to a vacuum with a confused student body that can't connect to the learning, and everything will need to be repeated later. If the students have already learned the content, the experience will be boring, and no new learning will take place. Either way, it leads to a waste of time and energy.

Targeted assessment is the principle behind the mastery challenges on Khan Academy and other learning software programs as well. As long as students have the attention span to persevere through them, the tests can give fairly accurate insight into students' understanding and gaps. If students don't have the attention span, and they randomly click or type answers, of course the data are no good. That's why it's helpful to have a human monitoring the process and to not expect too much testing time. Finding the balance is important.

If gaps are identified, it's important to have plans in place to close them. For classrooms, a teacher should plan what to do if it's a majority or a minority of the students with the gaps. With a minority, individual lessons and practice, perhaps with technology, can be assigned. With a majority, the whole class can receive reengagement into the concept. For homeschooled or tutored students, of course, their learning can be tailored to whatever the students need.

The good news about this is that generally, the older the students are, the faster they are able to close knowledge gaps. A major factor in this is their motivation: if they feel discouraged about math or their own abilities in it, this can cause a blockage to growth and putting in the necessary work. However, with encouragement and understanding the importance of challenge and closing gaps, students can learn and improve their skills rapidly.

A STRENGTH-BASED APPROACH

One of the best ways to do this is to use a strength-based approach. That is, even if students don't have the specific knowledge about the topic at hand, bringing up what they do know can help them make the necessary connections to make the leap.

Let's take, for example, multiplying two *binomials* (two algebraic terms making up an expression) together, say, $(x + 4)(-2x - 8)$. In many cases, teachers rely on *FOIL*, a mnemonic for multiplying the terms in order—"first, outside, inside, last"—and repetitive practice until the students have the ability as a skill. They may even be able to retrieve and perform it as adults, though some may struggle.

However, ask people *why* we do this and usually, the best response that can be expected is "Distributive property," or "We have to multiply every term by every other term." Anything beyond that usually gets a shrug. Add another complexity, like a binomial times a trinomial, and so forth, and students start to make more mistakes. The procedure can fall apart without a strong foundation.

Even many high school math teachers aren't aware that the distributive property is one that students can use and name as early as third grade, when learning multiplication. For example, some multiplication facts, such as five times a number, can be easy to learn. Others can be more challenging, such as 8×7. But using the distributive property makes it much more approachable. We can use our strengths to work on our challenges.

Let's see how this works. Another way to look at 8×7 is $(5 + 3) \times (5 + 2)$, since $8 = 5 + 3$ and $7 = 5 + 2$. To show this, draw a diagram with eight rows of circles and seven columns. Then draw a line between the fifth column and the last two, and another between the fifth row and the last three.

At this point, there is an array of 5×5, 5×2, 3×5, and 3×2, or 25, 10, 15, and 6. Adding them together—$25 + (10 + 15) + 6$, or $25 + 25 + 6$, or 56—gives access to this math fact. This is illustrated in Figure 8.1.

This may be clunky, and there are simpler ways to do it mentally, like $(8 \times 5) + (8 \times 2)$—but practice with breaking the numbers down visually, and transitioning to an area model with numbers, helps many students understand the process of what happens when distributing numbers.

Returning to the strength-based approach: when we share an example like this, it can help students see that yes, they do have experience with the distributive property, and it can be extended to multiplying polynomials, just substituting algebraic terms for integers. An integer is any whole number, positive or negative, including zero.

For example, given $(x + 2)(x + 5)$, students can substitute any number for x. Let's take $x = 5$. We know that $5 + 2 = 7$, and $5 + 5 = 10$; also, $7 \times 10 = 70$. If we draw it out as an area model, we can get $(5 \times 5) + (5 \times 5) + (2 \times 5) + (2 \times 5)$. We get the same answer! Students can then play with other values substituted for x and find out that it works much like the mental strategies they learned for multidigit multiplication in fourth grade.

Then as we saw in chapter 3, multiplying binomials also relates to how students learned to multiply mixed numbers with an area model in fifth grade. The area model as a tool, then later translated to the box model (because you can't have negative area) when negative numbers are introduced, helps students understand that the math is not new but is related to what they already know.

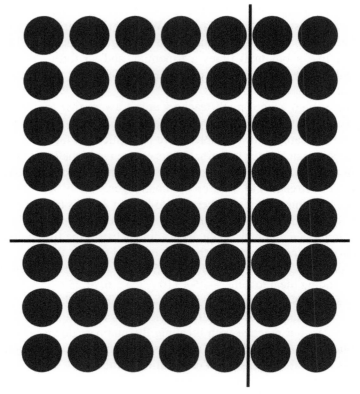

Figure 8.1.   An array showing the distributive property of multiplication.

KEEPING MATH CONNECTED AND RELEVANT

Another essential aspect is keeping the math relevant and connected. The older students get, the drier the teaching tends to be. And dry is boring. Shunting the teaching off to software is not a solution; screen time is exhausting in its own way, and it requires sitting and typing instead of engaging in communication and collaboration. Instead, teachers should find ways to bring in hands-on experiences, projects, and discussions of interesting questions to bring the math to life.

On the topic of bringing math to life, one question that comes up in almost every math class is, "How will I use this in real life?" A New York City school district put together a massive, thorough chart that shows well over one hundred professions, from accountant to X-ray technician, and the types of math they use regularly.[1] This can be an excellent resource to print and hang in the

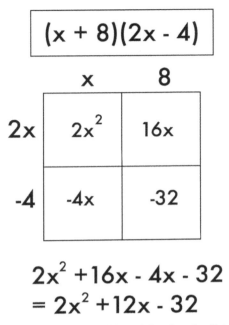

$$(x + 8)(2x - 4)$$

$$2x^2 + 16x - 4x - 32$$
$$= 2x^2 + 12x - 32$$

Figure 8.2. A box model for multiplying binomials using the distributive property.

classroom; when students ask when they would use that math, they can be invited to consult the chart and see for themselves.

In addition, one major challenge teachers face in maintaining class engagement these days is attention span. There is a lot of debate about what this means, but there is no doubt that devices such as cell phones present a greater temptation of interest than listening to a teacher speak about math, or a worksheet with math problems on it that may challenge one's thinking. Even without devices, adolescent interests tend to be more fun-focused and peer-focused than academic. Thus there is competition for the limited resources of student attention.

The listening community says that one way to increase attention span is through sparking curiosity. As Mark Twain says in *Tom Sawyer* (chapter 2), "Work consists of whatever a body is obliged to do, and Play consists of whatever a body is not obliged to do." Sparking curiosity makes the process of learning more like play than work.

When we are curious about something, particularly if it feels playful or like a game, we usually have the stamina to stay the course to find out about it, because it feels like fun and not work. These days we have been trained to find the answer to a question instantly through the devices at our fingertips, but that method doesn't answer everything. Witness the popularity of true crime shows that extend for multiple seasons.

How can we apply this approach to teaching math?

Some examples of interesting questions that could spark curiosity might be:

- Why is the unit circle named that? Where did it come from?
- How do transformations [in geometry] relate to what happens on a phone screen or a video game?
- What is calculus for?
- How did someone come up with the quadratic formula?
- How does factoring quadratics connect to finding factors of a composite number?
- How do they calculate a home run distance so quickly on TV? How do sabermetrics (advance statistics applied to baseball) work?
- What's the perfect parabola for an arch?

Part of this requires a rich teacher knowledge of how the math can be translated to hands-on or visual experiences. If one grew up enjoying the puzzle of math and performing mathematical procedures in school, or performed well in math class without needing to question deeply to understand it, there may be learning to do about this. One of the challenges presented in coaching teachers is when they enjoyed learning math for itself in school and don't find the need to find extra connections in it for those who don't experience it in the same way. It can be helpful for those with that background to speak with others who have struggled to understand in order to empathize with their points of view.

One way the author sparked curiosity in a student who didn't understand how a linear equation can help us draw a line was to compare it to a magic formula that unlocks the secrets of every point in the line. It's amazing; just put in any x-value, and the y-value will be revealed! This is different from just teaching the formula without meaning, keeping it as a mystery about how it works; this way brings an intrigue and interest into it.

For example, for $y = 3x + 8$, pick any x-value, say 12, and substitute it for x. The equation becomes $y = 3(12) + 8$, or $36 + 8$, or 44. So $x = 12$ and $y = 44$. Making a table of values with positive and negative values of x can allow a student to see how the line forms from these points, and whether they made any errors in calculation. The magic formula works!

Another example happened when a student was completely lost about combining like terms in the algebraic expression $4r + 5 - 6r - 8$. The author asked the student, "What do you like doing outside of school?" The student expressed an interest in video games. That led to the comparison of the r terms to game lives and the constant terms to game armor.

We wondered if we would have enough of each to finish out the level of this game. When we combined the same terms (lives with lives and game armor with game armor), we came up with $-2r - 3$, which showed we didn't have enough of either to make it to the next level; we would be down two lives and three pieces of armor.

Continued conversation like this with a gradual release of responsibility, to where the student was able to do the work on his own and check it with a peer, correcting his own misconceptions, led to a more durable understanding of these approaches.

How can a parent or teacher learn what they may be missing in their understanding of making more advanced math more hands on and relevant? Fortunately, there are resources to help with this.

A textbook called *Financial Algebra* by Robert Gerver and Richard Sgroi is one such resource.[2] This book integrates Algebra I, Algebra II, and geometry topics in a project-based and realism-based approach. Projects are encouraged, such as having students go to multiple car dealerships and get quotes on buying or leasing cars, after which they use mathematical functions to understand the pricing and get the best deals.

Along the same lines, there is a free financial algebra course available online at Next Gen Personal Finance, a site that is free now and promises to remain free forever.[3] It is also integrated with Desmos, for interactive, hands-on types of activities. There are nine-week courses and full-year courses, as well as a middle school course. These can be used by teachers, homeschooling parents, and more.

Another good resource can be found in free online curricula such as Illustrative Mathematics. There are several places to access this curriculum online, such as Open Up Resources.[4] The full curriculum is available here, with a teacher email address needed only to access the online assessment components, to prevent students from learning the answers in advance.

This resource includes integration with GeoGebra applets, meaning students can investigate concepts interactively in a structured way. There are also links to slideshows made by educators that guide the learning according to the lesson plan, saving that work for other educators. Many of the lessons include a list of materials needed to add the hands-on approach as well. Working through these lessons either alone, with students, or in a professional learning group can help an educator see how to engage students conceptually in higher-level math work.

HANDS ON IN HIGH SCHOOL

On that topic, revisiting the concept development approach shared through-out this book, the concrete-pictorial-abstract approach does not need to end in high school. While many teachers believe all math needs to be abstract at this level, this is not the case. The ideal situation is that students have mental models of the math concepts by the time they reach high school, and new math learning then causes them to retrieve those mental models, which the learning then builds upon and updates.

However, many students have incomplete mental models, and in some cases, they are introduced to new concepts that need new models. Even though they're older, they haven't ceased to learn in human ways; the concrete experience is what will help the learning be more memorable. What are some of the ways we can introduce the learning through hands-on approaches?

Using algebra tiles can be one way to underpin the learning. These can be used for everything from combining integers to factoring quadratics. Here is a starting point to understand them.

Algebra tiles are designed to work so that when multiplying a binomial with whole-number factors results in a perfect rectangle. Likewise, factoring a quadratic that is factorable to integer *coefficients* (the numbers that multiply the variables) allows one to create a rectangle and use the tiles to find side lengths. How do the pieces work?

To begin, the small square counters, with one side yellow (or any other color) and the other side red, represent a positive one and a negative one. They can be used to develop or refresh understanding of combining terms and using zero pairs, as described with the counters in the "Middle School" chapter. Operations with these—adding and subtracting, multiplying and dividing—can start students on the path of using them.

Next, the long, narrow rectangular pieces represent x, or a variable. You can add and subtract these with each other, but not with other pieces. The short side is the same length as the "one" pieces, and the long side is the same size as the next piece to be described.

The final piece in the kit is a square, with a side length the same as the long side of the x piece—making it x^2, or x-squared. For some students, and even some adults, that alone might create an aha moment!

How do we use these tiles for simplifying or factoring quadratic expressions? First, we need to understand that they only work for quadratics that involve integer factors, so they are good for initial conceptual introductions, but not for quadratics with fractional or complex factors. In other words, they will work for expressions like $(x + 3)(x + 2)$, or $x^2 + 5x + 6$, but not for expressions that don't factor evenly.

Figure 8.3.   An example of algebra tile manipulatives.

Let's have a look at the first example and how we might use it to find out the simplified version of the binomial factors. First, we can start with a mat where we place the factors as tiles along the top and left sides. The first factor, $x + 3$, is represented by the positive x-tile, and the three is represented by three positive one-tiles. We place these along the top—arbitrarily; since multiplication is commutative, they can go either place. Next, the $x + 2$ factor is constructed along the sides.

Now that both factors are in place, we can multiply. Where the two x-factors are, placing a positive x^2 tile between them shows that one side has a value of x, so the area of the sides multiplied is x^2. The square fits perfectly.

Next, we can multiply across. We have $(x \cdot 1)$ three times, so we place three x-tiles vertically next to the square tile and underneath the three one-tiles. Similarly, for the side factor, we put two x-tiles horizontally beneath the square tile. This leaves a blank area for our $2 \cdot 3$, so we can place six positive one-tiles there, completing the rectangle.

Counting all the tiles, we can see now that we have one x^2, five x-tiles, and six one-tiles. This shows us that our factors simplify to $x^2 + 5x + 6$.

What happens if we want to start with the simplified expression and find the factors? The same thing happens but in reverse, which can require some trial and error especially if any negative factors are involved.

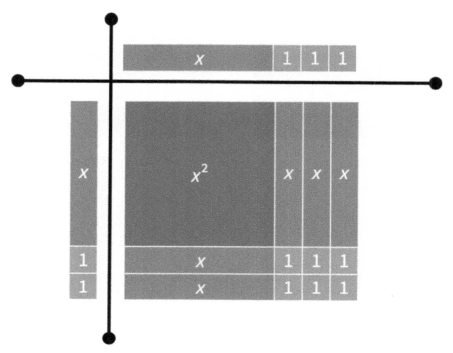

Figure 8.4.   An algebra tile model for multiplying two positive binomials. *Created using Polypad, found at polypad.org, part of Amplify.*

Let's try factoring $x^2 - x - 12$. Now we have two negative terms, so we have to think about how that will work with the tiles.

If you have algebra tiles or can use an online version,[5] try figuring it out with them yourself before coming back to guidance here.

Perhaps you got a bit stuck with the fact of the negative tiles. It might help to start with the square tile, and then in the lower right corner, start putting together the -12 out of negative one-tiles. Try different arrangements, adding the x-tiles along the top and left side until they add up to $-x$, with the whole arrangement forming a rectangle.

If you have solved the puzzle, you'll find that the x-factors are $3x$ and $-4x$. A question we can ask when factoring is, what are the factors of the constant term that add up to the coefficient of the middle term, in this case, negative one? Knowing the factors of 12 are 12 and 1, 2 and 6, and 3 and 4, only the last set have a difference of one between them; the 4 must be the negative factor, then, because the difference has to be negative. Figure 8.5 shows how the algebra tiles could be arranged to show this, or $(x + 3)(x - 4)$.

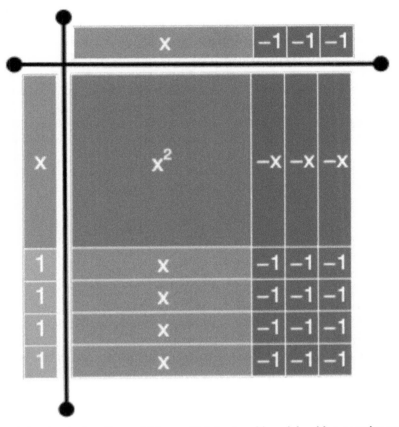

Figure 8.5. An algebra tile model for multiplying two binomials with a negative term. *Created using Polypad, found at polypad.org, part of Amplify.*

When students work with algebra in forms like this, it makes it more tangible and less abstract. Many adults have aha moments after working with these too, finally understanding the concepts behind the math.

This is just one example of how high school math can be hands on. In some cases, STEM (science, technology, engineering, and math) integration can fill in. For example, as students take high school chemistry and physics, they need to use many of the problem-solving skills learned in math. In chemistry, algebra can be used to balance chemical equations; since the number of atoms must remain the same on both sides, finding the coefficients for each molecule becomes less mysterious. There is a PhET simulation[6] that uses a balance scale to model this visually. The simulation uses balls to represent atoms and show when the molecules balance out.

Likewise, in physics, much of the math overlaps with high school math subjects: trigonometry, rate (velocity), and, for more advanced physics, calculus. The equations may use different variables and be more complex, but the concepts are the same. For example, one formula to find acceleration is $a = \Delta v / \Delta t$. That may look confusing, but it's just shorthand for "acceleration is the difference of velocity, or ending velocity minus starting velocity, divided by the time that elapsed, or ending time minus starting time."

So if a ball started falling at 20 feet per second and ended at 60 feet per second, and it started falling at 3:07:36 and ended at 3:08:18, acceleration would be 60 ft/s − 20 ft/s, or 40 ft/s, divided by 3:08:18 − 3:07:36 (a difference of $^{42}/_{60}$ of a second, or 0.7 seconds). Then 40 ft/s ÷ 0.7 s is 57.14 feet per square second acceleration. The equation looks like

$$\frac{\dfrac{(60-20)\,ft}{s}}{0.7s}.$$

Harkening back to chapter 7, this is another example of why a solid understanding of working with fractions is so important. At this point we can simplify and invert and multiply, to make $^{40ft}/_{1s} \times 1/_{0.7s} = ^{40}/_{0.7}{}^{ft}/_{s}$, or $57.14^{ft}/_{s}$. Yes, there are a number of symbols and fractions, but if we take our time to carefully read through it, it can make sense.

The connections between the topics can make the concepts behind each of them clearer to students. Alternatively, without a strong enough background and understanding of the concepts and how the math works, students can founder and find all the math and science subjects too difficult.

This last section was a bit more technical, and maybe it was challenging to work through. One benefit of this can be that when adults are challenged, it's a good reminder of how it feels to young people all the time when they meet new material. It takes work and energy to persevere, and there is nothing like the feeling when one is successful in this. Remember that an attitude of "I can't—*yet*" can help overcome the barriers that might otherwise defeat us.

In addition to general STEM integration, projects can inspire interest and focus. There is nothing like real-life problems that need solving to bring focus and interest. For example, at the start of the COVID-19 pandemic, interest in inexpensively cleaning air rose a great deal. In addition to the many expensive commercial air filters, home scientists started building and experimenting with air filters made of furnace filters, a box fan, duct tape, and cardboard. These Corsi-Rosenthal boxes turned out to be very effective, not only for reducing virus transmission, but also for helping provide breathable air as the smoke and pollution from forest fires became more prevalent. This is just one example of clever ways to address a modern problem that could interest students.

A possible approach to projects is to ask students to consider one of the problems facing the future. This will give some insight as to what they are thinking and will drive their interest in researching possible solutions. Once they have identified a problem and existing solutions, they can be guided into a project that will help them find the outcomes.

An example of a project could be researching cooling effectiveness. With the increased heat many areas are experiencing, modern forms of cooling with HVAC systems might have trouble keeping up, especially with increases in storms and power outages. Students might decide to try out a variety of cooling systems, from shading windows to geothermal models to green roofs. These can be built onto small-scale models and the temperature differences measured.

One way to test this could be by using a 3D printer to print a few different models of the same home and try different approaches to cooling them, or students can try designing their own home structures and seeing if some are better at staying cool than others. They can even put in different insulation materials. The options are endless. This type of thinking and exploration can also lead to future innovators and scientists, a wonderful math or science fair, and students who develop strong problem-solving approaches.

High school is a time of jumping off to adulthood. A student's outcomes here can set the tone for the rest of their life. Providing many opportunities for a connected and meaningful experience in math can allow a strong foundation for a lifetime of continued learning.

Important Practices

- Consider whether accelerating a student into an advanced track is beneficial in the long term.
- To ensure student success, assess existing competencies using benchmark assessments, and then close gaps as needed.
- When closing gaps, use prior knowledge to build capacity using a strength-based approach.
- Spark curiosity about math topics by sharing, and encouraging students to ask, questions that can be answered using mathematics.
- Keep the conversation about how math is relevant to real life going throughout math education.
- Wherever possible, incorporate the use of hands-on materials to explore new concepts and make connections to prior concepts.
- Integrate mathematics into other subjects, and make math integration explicit when learning other subjects.

- Use projects to investigate and explore all kinds of different mathematical applications.

What concepts stayed mysterious to you in high school, and what could you do to unlock them?

The author struggled with trigonometry; learning the relationships in the unit circle, and how they were derived, unlocked more understanding.

NOTES

1. Find the spreadsheet at https://tinyurl.com/mathjobsheet.

2. Robert K. Gerver and Richard J. Sgroi, *Financial Algebra: Advanced Algebra with Financial Applications* (Boston: Cengage, 2021).There is a website with additional resources at https://www.drrsgroi.com/.

3. The website address is https://www.ngpf.org/math/financial-algebra/.

4. One of several sources for Illustrative Mathematics is https://openupresources .org.

5. One source is https://mathigon.org/polypad#algebra-tiles, where these tile images come from (used with permission). Draw a corner frame using the drawing tools on the bottom, and then use the tiles on the left to model the expression.

6. Find the simulator at https://phet.colorado.edu/sims/html/balancing-chemical -equations/latest/balancing-chemical-equations_en.html.

Chapter 9

Interlude 2

A Bridge to the Future

Without mathematics, there's nothing you can do. Everything around you is mathematics. Everything around you is numbers.—Shakuntala Devi

What does success or failure in math mean? What implications does it have for adult life? This chapter explores the impacts math ability can have on a life going forward.

At this point in one's life, having finished high school, it's time to take on some adult responsibilities. The young person usually starts working or going to college. Along with many other capabilities, their achievements in math will determine, in part, how far and how easily the young person will travel from here.

Let's take students who had an ideal path. They had strong foundations in elementary school, middle school developed their more abstract thinking, and while they may have stumbled here and there, they have ended up with a deep enough understanding in math to excel in high school. They have the foundations to pursue a variety of courses, from becoming an electrician or an auto mechanic to entering college to train for careers as various as engineer to artist. When life throws challenges their way, they have a strong problem-solving ability and can think the challenges through. They can understand financial balances enough to manage and not accrue overwhelming debt.

More than that, they may have a love of math. They understand that math is everywhere around us: in the seasons, in the patterns of flowers, in the rhythms of the weather, in the distances to the stars. They may think about the days of the week and how to use their energy optimally to make the most of their life. They may contribute to discussions among their peers with critical thinking about whatever topic is being discussed, from politics to innovation. Like reading, math is a language they are fluent in and can use on a day-to-day basis without stress.

On the other hand, what about the students who fall off the journey to understanding math? Whether failed by a teacher or because they developed a mindset that caused them to believe they can't, they now leave high school disliking, dreading, and/or fearing math.

To begin, there was a study published in the United Kingdom in 2021, where students can opt to stop learning mathematics at age sixteen. Scientists studied the brains of those who continued studying math and those who stopped; the subjects were ages fourteen to eighteen.[1]

The results showed that in the prefrontal cortex, an essential chemical that keeps the brain flexible and growing was greatly reduced in those who stopped studying math. This area affects problem solving, memory, learning, and math itself. Before students stopped learning math, there was no difference in the levels of this chemical; the difference was also independent of intellectual ability.

In fact, the difference was so great that researchers could tell who stopped with math and who continued just by looking at the amount of this chemical in the person's brain. The amount of chemical also correlated highly with scores on math attainment tests about nineteen months later.

So those who stop studying math early are at a cognitive disadvantage against those who continue, even on a biological basis.

In addition, the twenty-first century is a world of data. Using data to understand our world is everywhere, from risk assessment about health and welfare, to what natural disasters are likely in a certain area and whether the equation of living there makes sense. Being able to take on financial risks, such as credit cards and loans, requires an understanding of cause, consequence, and problem solving. This is explored in more detail in chapter 10.

Mental fitness comes into play as well. As one student put it, working with mathematics is like a workout for your brain. Like muscles grow with pressure and the right kind of stress, brains stay fit with mental exercise. A number of mobile apps capitalize on this to help mental acuity improve, and mathematical activities are part of them. This helps the brain be fitter for employment that requires the use of math; these jobs and careers tend to pay better than those that don't.

Another student reflected that each subject we learn and study increases our opportunity to learn and to work. Conversely, each subject we do not study decreases our field of opportunity.

Fear of math due to feeling inadequate or not understanding it can lead to a lifetime of avoidance of the subject and thus, reduction of opportunity. Jo Boaler called this "psychological prisons" from which some people never escape, leading to, or reinforcing, social class inequalities.[2] Therefore, access to math understanding is a key part of improving equity, as well as access to better opportunities in life.

What examples can you find of how math can create or decrease opportunity?

A greater capability with math has led to the author's understanding and appreciation of fields outside of her expertise, such as astronomy and anthropology.

NOTES

1. "Lack of Math Education Negatively Affects Adolescent Brain and Cognitive Development: A New Study Suggests That Not Having Any Math Education after the Age of 16 Can Be Disadvantageous," ScienceDaily, June 7, 2021, www.sciencedaily .com/releases/2021/06/210607161149.htm.

2. Jo Boaler, "The 'Psychological Prisons' from Which They Never Escaped: The Role of Ability Grouping in Reproducing Social Class Inequalities," *Forum* 47, nos. 2 & 3 (2005): 135–44, https://doi.org/10.2304/forum.2005.47.2.2.

Chapter 10

Adulthood

Relevance or Erosion

Being an adult means never having to show your work on math problems.—Darynda Jones

We've seen in previous chapters that a good relationship with math and strong conceptual understanding are essential for success in school. They also provide access to a number of other understandings that make a difference in understanding the world. What about in adulthood?

Like in the other stages of life, adulthood comes with many challenges that many people find surprising, unexpected, or hard to cope with. Most adults had many years of mostly academic schooling that didn't offer too many life skills. Classroom life doesn't mirror workplace life, and even brief internships don't bring the full experience of the interminable nature of needing to work for a living and the challenges that brings.

Our journeys with math, along with everything else we learn, become part of our toolbox for navigating life. We understand this with reading and writing (literacy); even if we don't become big readers as adults, we use them every day in navigating life, media, forms, and so on. If because of a less than optimal personal journey with math, what we learned becomes only as useful as a rusty hammer, we can only pass on a rusty hammer to our students.

Having a vision of how math can be useful into adulthood can help our students, and maybe ourselves, embrace the concept of being lifelong learners. This makes the content of our education in school only the beginning, allowing us to upgrade to math "power tools" over time. We can then use our improved tools in our lives and work; we can also pass them on to our students, our children, and our friends or colleagues.

If our experiences have been good and enjoyable, and we are happy with how we use math in our lives, wonderful! There is a lot earlier in this book that can deepen and enrich one's relationship with math and how one supports the math journeys of the children in our lives, whether our own or in our classrooms. This chapter can also offer additional perspectives on how math can be useful into adulthood, perhaps opening new avenues for the reader.

However, with a large percentage of adults experiencing math anxiety or even math phobia, this chapter is designed to support the adult journey toward improving one's relationship with math—toward relevancy and away from erosion.

Why now, though, at the end of this book? For some people, their math anxiety is so severe that even if they get excited about the learning possibilities in this book, they may think they may not be the person to provide support for children. This chapter supports changing these patterns of thinking for those people, with one more opportunity to encourage growth mindset and the belief that one can do it.

ADULTHOOD AND MATH: CONSIDERING THE ISSUES

Like any other habit, a habit of mind takes many attempts to unlearn or replace. Each chapter in this book offers a different perspective, a different angle, and a different opportunity to change one's habit of resistance to math, if it exists.

Why is this important? After all, we have all gotten as far as we have, and most people are doing well as functioning adults. Depending on our age, though, we may still be struggling to develop certain competencies. Those who don't pursue careers in mathematically related fields such as engineering, architecture, accounting, or teaching math often forget as much math as they can after they leave school. The erosion of their understanding of math may not have much of an impact if the math was taught as a series of formulas to memorize. However, if math was taught and experienced with meaning and connection, its benefits can influence many areas of life for the better. Let's take a look at some examples of where better numeracy, or the ability to understand and work with numbers, can be helpful or necessary in adult life.

An obvious one is financial planning. Credit cards, retirement planning, taxes, salary, and benefits—all require numeracy to manage well. On the other side, adults who find these areas difficult often rely on others to guide them, which can leave them open to unscrupulous manipulation, embezzlement, and more. As was mentioned before, one participant in an early workshop broke down in tears because she had so much trauma related to math. This impacted her ability to manage finances, leaving her destitute and struggling in her forties; she saw the possibilities if that hadn't happened, and the gap between her reality and what could have been was painful to her.

We don't want this outcome for our young people, so how can we help them avoid it? Let's take credit cards as an example. To rent an apartment, buy a house or car, and more, one needs to have a decent credit score. So college students, and other young people straight out of high school, are encouraged to start building credit right away.

However, students tend to see the low minimum payments and the benefits such as points on card agreements without understanding the high fees and interest rates, and salespeople are trained to emphasize only the benefits. If during their young adulthood, they lose a job, overspend, or otherwise find themselves unable to pay off the monthly balance, they can find themselves mired in an ever-increasing pile of debt, as the interest on their balance due increases, and past-due bills accrue additional fees. Eventually their credit score may plummet, leading to a catch-22 of being unable to find decent employment as well. The consequences of these events can last well into older adult life.

This doesn't even touch on the issue of student debt. Often after years or even decades of paying large amounts monthly, people end up owing more than when they first took out the loan. High college tuition means lack of equity of access, due to the financial divide between those who can afford college due to generational wealth, and those who would be saddled by an unmanageable debt load if they took it on.

Having strong numerical sense and guidance means young people beginning adulthood can assess risk more accurately and make more informed choices. For example, even though it may not be their first choice, they might decide to go to community college for two years and then transfer to their school of choice, lightening their future debt and perhaps qualifying for a better scholarship due to a strong academic record.

For credit cards, a person might use a particular online store a lot, so they choose the store card, but they only charge as much as they know they can pay off in a month, tracking their spending carefully. Then instead of redeeming the rebate on "free" items from that store, they continue to charge items to the card and redeem the rebate in payments to the card or cash, understanding that they would lose points, and therefore cash, by redeeming the points for stuff.

The list goes on and on: when numbers aren't overwhelming or anxiety producing, a person can be more thoughtful and deliberate in financial decision-making, which takes less time and energy out of one's life and can lead to a better quality of life overall.

Numbers affect many other areas of adult life as well; in fact, "adulting" can be seen through the lens of numbers, at least in part, in almost every area. Better numeracy can make these areas easier. Here are some examples:

- Cooking: How do I double or halve a recipe with fractional measurements? How will changing this or that proportion of ingredients change the outcome of the taste or texture? What about cooking time or temperature?
- Gardening: How far is far enough apart to plant seeds or plants? What do they need for optimal growth? How much sunlight, shade, water?
- Dining out: The menu has prices for each item, but how much will the final bill actually be after taxes and tip? Will the total stress the household budget? How do we split a complicated bill with a group at a restaurant? (This is one place where numerical prowess can really shine!)
- Following from the previous point—*is* there a household budget? How do we create one? What makes sense? How do we create sensible goals in our budget and achieve life balance with one? How do we track it?
- Shopping: What food can we afford? Which is more economical, the ingredients or the premade version? What is my balance of time versus money? What clothing is necessary and will last long enough for our needs?
- Cars: At what point is it a better choice to buy a used car instead of a new one? At which point does it stop being worth repairing an old car, meaning it's time to replace it instead?
- Hobbies: A fellow writer shared a story about how she started using math she'd never thought she'd use again after she left her work in information technology. When she started knitting, she discovered many knitting patterns that she liked but needed adjusting. Although it's possible to get hit-or-miss results by following the pattern as written, since every knitter's stitch width (known as "gauge") is different, patterns should be adjusted to the proportion of stitches per inch the knitter uses—a ratio problem, or a proportion. Then if one wishes to design one's own patterns or adapt existing patterns to more exact measurements of the body that the sweater, hat, and so forth is for, more complex equations are needed. There are some books that help with these calculations, but it's easier and more intuitive if one understands and can apply the math oneself.
- Athletics: What is the optimal angle at which to shoot the ball into the hoop or goal? How much practice is best before injuries are likely? And then, of course, there are sports statistics, fantasy football leagues, and much more.

Now that we've seen some of the extensive ways numeracy can be helpful to competent adult life, what other doors can a successful relationship with math open?

A major part of adult life is making sense of information presented by the media and making decisions about it. When numeracy allows a person to understand research and statistics, it's much less likely that their decisions will be swayed by false or skewed information. Data makes sense and allows one to make an informed decision, in voting, health, where to live, salary negotiations, and much more. These elements contribute to critical thinking ability about the world around us.

In addition, a strong understanding of math can leave one settled in the face of chaos. Children these days experience so much anxiety and uncertainty about the future; a strong grasp of math is one tool they can use to navigate turbulent waters. While human patterns don't always follow measurable cycles, there is a cyclical nature to human behavior, war and peace, that can be observed as from a distance, allowing one to avoid being swept into intense reactions to difficult news and contribute constructively.

Problem solving is another skill that strong math ability can support. Everyone deals with problems all the time, from appliances or vehicles that break down, to loss of electricity, to the effects of storms, illness, and more. The ability to solve problems can help one keep a cool head in the face of a crisis.

SOLUTIONS

What are some of the solutions for those who find themselves saddled with an inherited fear or dislike of math that is hampering them in life? This section will include a number of ideas that may or may not apply to a certain individual; please take what applies and leave the rest.

1. Therapy. Whether with a therapist or on one's own, in some cases identifying and healing the trauma of past experiences with math may be part of the way forward. A math teacher from one's school years may have been mean, or bigoted against one's gender, or more interested in showing off what they know than teaching the students, or may have just allowed students to hide their lack of understanding while the gaps between what they knew and what they should know grew wider and wider. Some teachers hate math themselves and express that either directly or indirectly, influencing their students. Some people may have been homeschooled by a parent who didn't know math well, so they identify with that. Some never had a teacher who could teach them in a way they understood. Some had a school or teacher who equated math with worksheets, making math feel boring and useless.

    Whatever the reason, identifying it and starting to retell the story of it in oneself can help. First, one must understand that the dislike of math isn't the person's fault. It's a sign of a faulty heritage with math. Then one can decide what kind of relationship one wants to have with math, in which case some of the following suggestions may be helpful.

2. Connecting math with nature. Being with nature, in general, can be healing and regulating for our systems. Deliberately choosing to be in nature and discovering as many numbers and patterns as one can could be a start in retelling the story of numbers in oneself. Chapter 4 may help with this. One example is looking at a nautilus shell sliced lengthwise, and seeing the amazing repeated proportions in that, named by mathematicians since ancient times the golden ratio.

3. Connect math with art.
   - Drawing mandalas can be meditative and peaceful, and they involve geometry, patterns, and numbers of repeats.
   - Perspective in drawing or painting uses geometry as well.
   - Explore fractal patterns.
   - Make mosaics or tessellations.
   - Identify the beats per minute in a song you love.
   - If you enjoy a painting, see if there is something mathematical in it that causes that experience: proportions, patterns, certain shapes. . . .
   - Look at buildings and paintings that were made with the golden ratio in mind, and see how those make you feel.
   - Watch videos and shows like Vihart's "Doodling in Math Class" YouTube series and the crime drama called *Numb3rs*.
   - If you love to read, many fun books that incorporate math are out there. Abakcus.com has a nice list.[1] An internet search on your specific genre, such as "math romance novels," can bring up other options.

Close up your own knowledge gaps. Learning doesn't end when school does. Sometimes we didn't do well with Greek mythology or Shakespeare or calculus in school because we weren't ready for them, but now we are. Free online resources like Khan Academy can provide a self-paced, quiet, customized experience where you can practice math, starting wherever you are and going wherever your destination may be. Want to learn about percentages better? It may take you through some fraction work first, and then you'll see how they relate to percentages. You'll practice until you're proficient. Want to understand calculus, because you weren't ready for it in high school or college? Maybe you need refreshing in working with polynomials first, and you work your way up to differential equations. While you're there, maybe you notice the course on computer programming and decide to learn about HTML and JavaScript. There are so many possibilities!

Mindset can be a good way forward. Consider replacing "I can't" with "I'm not able to *yet*." Kind of like "fake it till you make it," use the strategies you can use to encourage students: rather than giving up, *pretend* you can, or imagine you are doing it. It can even help to metaphorically walk in another's footsteps: that is, think of someone who is or was skilled at the process you're attempting, and pretend you are them. You might be surprised at how much confidence you develop and how much easier it becomes! And don't forget to give yourself time. Rushing or expecting instant results is almost a guarantee of failure.

Important Practices

- Think about ways you use math in your life already, and use those to boost your confidence about it.
- Examine the roots of any lack of confidence in math, and realize they are not about you.
- Find ways to make math enjoyable and connected to meaning in your life.
- Be a lifelong learner; take some time to become proficient in something school failed to teach you, if you want to learn it.
  - Connect to the math all around us. Revisit chapter 4 to think and wonder about the patterns in nature; confirm or try to disprove them. If you wish, find a way to fall in love with numbers and what they represent.
  - Learn to use a spreadsheet program, such as Google Sheets. Many free tutorials exist online, or you can hire a tutor—including, possibly, a young person.
  - Learn to create a budget. Maybe this can be your goal when learning to use the spreadsheet program. Visit a local library to get suggestions on good books to get you started. Perhaps they will even offer a class!
  - Get to understand loans, investing, interest, and compound interest. The Next Gen Personal Finance course isn't only for high schoolers; there's a lot in there for adults as well.[2]
- Always keep mindset in mind! The philosophy of "not yet" will serve you well.

What do you wonder about math in adulthood?
The author wonders how math became such a difficult subject for so many people.

NOTES

1. See https://abakcus.com/15-beautiful-math-inspired-novels-for-math-lovers/.
2. The website is https://www.ngpf.org/curriculum/.

Glossary

addend: one number that is being added to another.

array: objects or drawings arranged in rows and columns.

benchmark fraction: a fraction that can be used to compare the values of other fractions. Examples include one-half, one-fourth, and three-fourths.

binomial: an expression adding or subtracting two terms.

coefficient: a number multiplying a variable.

commutative property: a property that applies to addition and multiplication, in which the order of the terms being added or multiplies doesn't matter; it gives the same result.

composite number: a counting number that has multiple factors—itself, one, and other whole numbers.

concrete, pictorial (or representational), abstract: the sequence of introducing a math concept that begins with a hands-on activity, then a 2D representation of that experience, followed by a pencil-and-paper abstract representation of both, which can be a symbol, an operation, an algorithm, and more.

differentiation: a teaching practice that involves ensuring that all students are able to approach the learning with strategies and tools that make sense to them.

distributive property: the full name is the "distributive property of multiplication over addition." That is, when multiplying a number by two numbers added together, the result is the same as multiplying the number by each individual number and adding them together. See the area model examples for a visual representation of this.

domain and range: in an algebraic function, the domain represents the set of independent values, usually graphed on the x-axis; the range is set of values the function produces, usually graphed on the y-axis.

equation: two or more expressions or numbers, of equal value, separated by an equal sign. An analogy is a balance scale in which both sides weigh the same amount but may be different objects.

expression: a math "sentence" with at least two numbers or variables and at least one mathematical operation between them.

factor: a whole number that can be multiplied to get another number; when dividing, one of the results from the division problem.

FOIL: a mnemonic for the distributive property to recall an order of multiplying two binomials: multiply the first terms in each, then the outside (first and last) terms in each, the inside (last and first) terms in each, and the last (last and last). It reminds students to multiply every term by every other term.

identity property of addition: the sum of any value or variable and zero is the same value or variable; e.g., $x+0=x$.

identity property of multiplication: the product of any value or variable and one is the same value or variable; e.g., $x \cdot 1 = x$.

integer: a number that is not a fraction, which includes all positive numbers, negative numbers, and zero.

minuend: in a subtraction situation, the number from which to subtract another—or the "whole" in a part-whole representation.

partitive division: dividing a whole into equal parts.

polynomial: a mathematical expression that involves multiple variable and constant (number) terms.

portfolio: a collection of a student's best or representative schoolwork, used in some schools as an alternative means of assessment and/or for student-guided parent conferences.

prime number: a counting number that can only be divided by itself and one.

product: the result of multiplying two or more numbers together.

productive struggle: an approach in teaching that encourages effort in learning, leading to intellectual work and accomplishment, particularly in problem solving.

quadratic: in expressions and equations, with the highest term (variable) having a power of two.

quotative division: also known as "division by fitting," this is finding how many of a certain size equal parts fit into a certain whole.

quotient: the result of a division problem or situation.

Say Ten counting: a method of counting that mirrors that of certain Asian languages, in which place value is represented in the count. That is, instead of, "Eleven, twelve, thirteen," etc., the count would go, "Ten-one, ten-two, ten-three," etc. Chapter 3 has more on this.

scaffolding: the process of providing support for students that is appropriate for their individual learning needs.

schematic visualization: a type of visual representation of the mathematics in a situation.

subtrahend: in a subtraction situation, the number being subtracted from another.

synaptic pruning: a process by which the brain reduces the number of unused neurons and neural connections in the brain to make its processing more efficient.

trinomial: an algebraic expression of the sum or difference of three terms.

unit fraction: one countable unit of a fractional size, such as one half, one fifth, etc.

variable: a symbol, usually a letter, representing an unknown quantity or quantities in an expression or equation.

zone of proximal development (ZPD): coined by Lev Vygotsky, this is the level of difficulty in learning that is not too easy and not so challenging that it's frustrating, but it creates opportunities to learn and grow.

Bibliography

Boaler, Jo. "The 'Psychological Prisons' from Which They Never Escaped: The Role of Ability Grouping in Reproducing Social Class Inequalities." *Forum* 47, nos. 2 & 3 (2005): 135–44. https://doi.org/10.2304/forum.2005.47.2.2.

Boaler, Jo, Lang Chen, Cathy Williams, and Montserrat Cordero. *Seeing as Understanding: The Importance of Visual Mathematics for Our Brain and Learning.* Youcubed, Stanford University. 2017. https://www.youcubed.org/wp-content/uploads/2017/03/Visual-Math-Paper-vF.pdf.

Brown, Peter C., Henry L. Roediger III, and Mark A. McDaniel. *Make It Stick: The Science of Successful Learning.* Cambridge, MA: Belknap Press of Harvard University Press, 2014.

Bruner, Jerome. "The Course of Cognitive Growth." *American Psychologist* 19, no. 1 (1964): 1–15. https://doi.org/10.1037/h0044160.

Charles A. Dana Center. *Launch Years: A New Vision for the Transition from High School to Postsecondary Mathematics.* Austin: University of Texas, 2020. https://www.utdanacenter.org/sites/default/files/2020-03/Launch-Years-A-New-Vision-report-March-2020.pdf.

Clotfelter, Charles T., Helen F. Ladd, and Jacob L. Vigdor. "The Aftermath of Accelerating Algebra: Evidence from District Policy Initiatives." *Journal of Human Resources* 50, no. 1 (2015): 159–88. http://www.jstor.org/stable/24735411.

Common Core Standards Writing Team. *Progressions for the Common Core State Standards for Mathematics.* Tucson: Institute for Mathematics and Education, University of Arizona, 2022. https://mathematicalmusings.org/wp-content/uploads/2023/02/Progressions.pdf.

Dweck, Carol S. *Mindset: The New Psychology of Success: How We Can Learn to Fulfill Our Potential.* New York: Random House, 2006.

Fischer, Charles Ames. *The Power of the Socratic Classroom.* N.p.: Sienna Books, 2019.

Fletcher, Graham. "Teaching Keywords? Forget about It!" *Questioning My Metacognition* (blog). January 12, 2015. https://gfletchy.com/2015/01/12/teaching-keywords-forget-about-it/.

Forsten, Char, and Torri Richards. *Math Talk: Teaching Concepts & Skills through Illustrations & Stories.* Peterborough, NH: Crystal Springs Books, 2009.

Gerver, Robert K., and Richard J. Sgroi. *Financial Algebra: Advanced Algebra with Financial Applications*. Boston: Cengage, 2021.

Gottlieb, Jacqueline, Manuel Lopes, and Pierre-Yves Oudeyer. "Motivated Cognition: Neural and Computational Mechanisms of Curiosity, Attention, and Intrinsic Motivation." *Advances in Motivation and Achievement* 19 (2016): 149–72. https://doi.org/10.1108/s0749-742320160000019017.

Grey, Peter. "Research Reveals Long-Term Harm of State Pre-K Program." *Psychology Today*, 2022. https://www.psychologytoday.com/us/blog/freedom -learn/202201/research-reveals-long-term-harm-state-pre-k-program.

Guth, Lisa M., and Stephen M. Roth. "Genetic Influence on Athletic Performance." *Current Opinion in Pediatrics* 25, no. 6 (2013): 653–58. https://doi.org/10.1097/ mop.0b013e3283659087.

Kastner, Bernice. *The Role of Language in Teaching Children Math*. Chicago: Austin Macauley, 2019.

Khan, Salman. *The One World Schoolhouse: Education Reimagined.* London: Hodder & Stoughton, 2012.

Le Corre, Mathieu, Gretchen Van de Walle, Elizabeth M. Brannon, and Susan Carey. "Re-visiting the Competence/Performance Debate in the Acquisition of the Counting Principles." *Cognitive Psychology* 52, no. 2 (2006): 130–69. https://doi .org/10.1016/j.cogpsych.2005.07.002.

Liang, Jian-Hua, Paul E. Heckman, and Jamal Abedi. "What Do the California Standards Test Results Reveal about the Movement Toward Eighth-Grade Algebra for All?" *Educational Evaluation and Policy Analysis* 34, no. 3 (September 2012): 328–43. https://edsource.org/wp-content/uploads/old/Algebra-CST -UCDavisStudy0812121.pdf.

Pearse, Margie. "Word Problems Are More Than Magic." *Corwin Connect* (blog). May 11, 2016. https://corwin-connect.com/2016/05/word-problems-magic/.

Pixner, Silvia, Verena Dresen, and Korbinian Moeller. "Differential Development of Children's Understanding of the Cardinality of Small Numbers and Zero." *Frontiers in Psychology* 9 (2018). https://doi.org/10.3389/fpsyg.2018.01636.

Powell, Katie. *Boredom Busters: Transform Worksheets, Lectures, and Grading into Engaging, Meaningful Learning Experiences*. Vancouver, WA: Dave Burgess Consulting, 2019.

Rosenthal, Robert, and Lenore Jacobson. "Pygmalion in the Classroom." *Urban Review* 3, no. 1 (1968): 16–20. https://doi.org/10.1007/bf02322211.

Sakai, Jill. "How Synaptic Pruning Shapes Neural Wiring during Development and, Possibly, in Disease." *Proceedings of the National Academy of Sciences* 117, no. 28 (2020): 16096–99. https://doi.org/10.1073/pnas.2010281117.

Schwartz, Richard Evan. *You Can Count on Monsters: The First 100 Numbers and Their Characters.* Providence, RI: American Mathematical Society, 2015.

Schwartz, Sarah. "California Adopts Controversial New Math Framework. Here's What's in It." Education Week. July 18, 2023. www.edweek.org/teaching-learning /california-adopts-controversial-new-math-framework-heres-whats-in-it/2023/07.

———. "Why Elite College Admissions May Play an Outsized Role in K–12 Math Programs." Education Week. September 20, 2022. www.edweek.org/teaching

-learning/why-elite-college-admissions-may-play-an-outsized-role-in-k-12-math
-programs/2022/09.

ScienceDaily. "Lack of Math Education Negatively Affects Adolescent Brain and Cognitive Development: A New Study Suggests That Not Having Any Math Education after the Age of 16 Can Be Disadvantageous." June 7, 2021. www .sciencedaily.com/releases/2021/06/210607161149.htm.

Smith, Margaret S., and Mary Kay Stein. *The Five Practices for Orchestrating Productive Mathematics Discussions*. 2nd ed. Reston, VA: National Council of Teachers of Mathematics, 2018.

Tau, Gregory Z., and Bradley S Peterson. "Normal Development of Brain Circuits." *Neuropsychopharmacology* 35, no. 1 (2009): 147–68. https://doi.org/10.1038/npp .2009.115.

Van de Walle, John A. *Elementary School Mathematics: Teaching Developmentally*. 2nd ed. New York: Longman, 1994.

Van Garderen, Delinda, Amy Scheuermann, and Christa Jackson. "Examining How Students with Diverse Abilities Use Diagrams to Solve Mathematics Word Problems." *Learning Disability Quarterly* 36, no. 3 (2012): 145–60. https://doi.org /10.1177/0731948712438558.

Van Garderen, Delinda, Amy Scheuermann, and Apryl Poch. "Challenges Students Identified with a Learning Disability and as High-Achieving Experience When Using Diagrams as a Visualization Tool to Solve Mathematics Word Problems." *ZDM: The International Journal on Mathematics Education* 46, no. 1 (July 30, 2013): 135–49. https://doi.org/10.1007/s11858-013-0519-1.

Witzel, Bradley S., Cecil D. Mercer, and M. David Miller. "Teaching Algebra to Students with Learning Difficulties: An Investigation of an Explicit Instruction Model." *Learning Disabilities Research and Practice* 18, no. 2 (2003): 121–31. https://doi.org/10.1111/1540-5826.00068.

Zwiers, Jeff, Jack Dieckmann, Sara Rutherford-Quach, Vinci Daro, Renae Skarin, Steven Weiss, and James Malamut. *Principles for the Design of Mathematics Curricula: Promoting Language* and *Content Development.* Understanding Language/Stanford Center for Assessment, Learning and Equity at Stanford University. 2017. https://ul.stanford.edu/sites/default/files/resource/2021-11/ Principles%20for%20the%20Design%20of%20Mathematics%20Curricula_1.pdf.

About the Author

Susan Midlarsky is an author, international teacher trainer, and passionate advocate for joy and satisfaction in learning. Having spent many years in the classroom prior to consulting, she became known for the creativity and fun she brought to learning, as well as the depth and breadth of her academic teaching. Her turning point in teaching math came early in her career by way of teaching the Singapore way, which led to a more meaningful understanding of math for herself. She was then able to bring that to her students.

Having found her strengths in teaching this way, she became a national trainer for various Singapore-guided math programs. That eventually led to joining the team that wrote the original Eureka Math curriculum. Working on that project, spanning more than a year, was a deep and thorough immersion into learning about how children learn math and how best to support them.

Later, Susan began consulting full-time, as well as continuing to work with students of all ages. She has coached public and private school teachers around the world, from the US Virgin Islands to China, but primarily in New York City. She has also worked in the homeschooling community as a teacher. Every student teaches her something new about how people learn.

Susan has been a writer for most of her life as well. She helped to develop the National Novel Writing Month's Young Writers' Program and has worked on several math and literacy education curricula and assessment programs. She loves to write and bring new understandings to others through the magic of language.

Find out more about Susan at susanmidlarsky.com.

Milton Keynes UK
Ingram Content Group UK Ltd.
UKHW012006040424
440634UK00016B/146